LIFE AND WITNESS OF
ST. IAKOVOS OF EVIA

LIFE AND WITNESS OF ST. IAKOVOS OF EVIA

Dr. Nicholas Baldimtsis

Uncut Mountain Press

LIFE AND WITNESS OF ST. IAKOVOS OF EVIA
© 2023
Uncut Mountain Press

All rights reserved under International and Pan-American Copyright Conventions.

uncutmountainpress.com

Cover Artwork: George Weis

Scriptural quotations are primarily taken from the New King James Version. The translator has emended some quotations to better reflect the original Greek text.

Library of Congress Cataloging-in-Publication Data
Baldimtsis, Dr. Nicholas

Life and Witness of St. Iakovos of Evia.—1st ed.
Translated by Fr. Nicholas Metrakos.

ISBN: 978-1-63941-017-0

I. Orthodox Christian Church
II. Orthodox Christian Hagiography

"Christ is always inside of me."

TABLE OF CONTENTS

Translator's Introduction 9

Introduction to the Greek 13

Chapter 1: Origin & Childhood Years 15

Chapter 2: The Elder's Life in the Military 37

Chapter 3: The Monastic Life of the Elder 45

Chapter 4: The Priestly Life of the Elder 59

Chapter 5: Stories & Visions of Father Iakovos 77

St. Iakovos (Tsalikis) of Evia - Reposed November 21st 1991, Commemorated November 22nd

TRANSLATOR'S INTRODUCTION

All Orthodox Christians are called to be translators. As the recipients of a living and life-giving Tradition we are called to drink from the same streams of grace, generation after generation, and bring forth spiritual fruits in our hearts and in our own lives. To live in the continuity of Tradition is to live the "life of the Holy Spirit in the Church, communicating to each member of the Body of Christ the faculty of hearing, of receiving, of knowing the Truth in the Light which belongs to it."[1] As we hear, receive and come to know the Truth, then we are also obliged to speak this Truth in our own words and in our own language as far as we are able.

The residents of the saint-bearing land of Asia Minor were expert translators. More importantly, they accurately translated from age to age in a context that was far from ideal. Within the family of St. Iakovos of Evia there were generations of holy people drinking from the river of Tradition, passing down an inheritance from parent to child. They never altered the meaning of what they learned but by allowing Christ to live in them authentically they produced their own "translations" of Holy Tradition.

---

[1] Lossky, Vladimir, *The Mystical Theology of the Eastern Church*, (Crestwood: St. Vladimir's Seminary Press, 1997), p. 152. (Translator's Note, hereafter abbreviated as "TN".)

As a minority population, the Romans of Asia Minor were relatively safe until the turn of the 20th century when the rise of a nationalistic Turkish state spelled the end of their legacy. Following the Treaty of Lausanne, the forced exile of the Orthodox Christians from Asia Minor, Pontus, and Eastern Thrace back to Greece in 1923 was called an "Exchange of Populations." In reality it was nothing short of a genocide: forced marches, abductions of fathers and brothers, and bloodshed. The family of St. Iakovos was not spared this cruelty.

Looking at the past we must not allow the feelings of injustice to consume our thoughts although certainly these holy people were not deserving of such inhumanity. Now standing almost 100 years after this tragic episode, the people of Asia Minor seem to speak collectively as a new Joseph, saying, "You meant evil against me; but God meant it for good, in order to bring it about as it is this day, to save many people alive."[2] Through the tragedy of this period, the rest of the world was made rich through the spiritual treasures these people brought with them both literally, as in the relics of St. John the Russian, and figuratively, in the legacy of this land's holy people.

Through saints like Paisios of the Holy Mountain and Sophia of Kleisoura we have been given a bridge to access this rich legacy. In the English-speaking world, another bridge through St. Iakovos of Evia has already been extended through the book *The Garden of the Holy Spirit* by Professor Stylianos Papadopoulos. We offer an additional view of the life of St Iakovos: a raw glimpse into the Elder's life in Asia Minor and his experiences as a boy, a priest-monk, and finally as an abbot—told in his own voice and in his own way.

---

2   Genesis 50:20.

In reading this translation and imbibing the grace-filled life of the saint, we should challenge ourselves to think about how we will translate this text in our own lives:

> How will each of us translate the divine language heard, known, and spoken by St. Iakovos—the Tradition of the Orthodox Church?

10 November 2021
+St. Arsenios the Cappadocian

Dr. Nicholas Baldimtsis with St. Iakovos

INTRODUCTION TO THE GREEK

The biographers of saints need to be saints themselves, therefore I never thought to write down the things God allowed me to learn from the righteous ascetic Fr. Iakovos. I met him when God, through the intercessions of St. David, allowed me to offer some medical care to the ascetic's very sick and tortured body. But the insistence, or rather spiritual command, of several pious believers pushed me to attempt to write down everything that follows. This of course is beneficial for myself, but also for my Christian brothers and sisters who will read the spiritual life and the supernatural events that I will try to narrate by the prayers of St. David and the Holy Elder Iakovos.

Icon of St. Iakovos

CHAPTER 1
Origin & Childhood Years

Asia Minor, which gave birth to so many saints of our Church, was also the homeland of our venerable Fr. Iakovos. The village where he was born and lived for the first two years of his life was Livisi, Makris, one of the coastal villages of the area around Ionia which is approximately the same latitude as Rhodes. The family of the Elder was one of the more well-to-do families of the village, and in addition to their fields they also had a house on their property. Their greatest wealth, however, was their piety, which stemmed from their deep-rooted, pure Christian faith. His family tree boasted in Christ[3] seven generations of hieromonks, one bishop, and a saint.

Perhaps at the end of this very deep ascetical Christian tradition, God knows, its greatest expression may be found: the last, holy branch of this spiritual vine; the venerable Fr. Iakovos.

The Elder was born in 1920 and at the age of two, with the terrible events of the Asia Minor Catastrophe, God allowed the uprooting of Hellenism from that holy earth. The Elder's family was forced to abandon their village and the Elder was transplanted like a precious and sanctified vine, to Amfissa and the village of Agios Georgios for

---
3   Galatians 6:14.

two years and afterwards to the village of Farakla, on the northern part of the island of Evia. There the Elder lived until he was 30 years old, when he was transplanted finally to the holy monastery of St. David.[4]

The saint's pious and ascetical mother Theodora played a foundational role in determining the course of his life. She was especially adorned with the virtues of almsgiving, continence (fasting and modesty), a good work ethic, and maintaining a good home. These virtues were planted with love and patience in the soft soul of her favorite child Iakovos. Fr. Iakovos would say that his mother had the soul of a nun. Despite her monastic demeanor, according to the tradition of their region, her parents engaged her to be married (without asking her opinion) at the age of twelve to the Elder's father. They were married when she was eighteen. His mother's virginal soul was ashamed because she did not have any worldly, carnal desires. In light of this, her family became involved and encouraged her (to put it nicely—they actually beat her) to live like a "natural" wife and spouse. From their marriage was born many children—about eight—but God only allowed only three to survive. The Elder was the second of the children who were "the leftovers of Charos"[5] as his mother often referred to her living children. Fr. Iakovos was the second boy, followed by his little and only sister.

---

4 Like St. Iakovos, St. David of Evia (November 1) was called to dedicate his life to God from a young age by St. John the Baptist himself. He became a monk at the age of 15. Leaving his first monastery, he was accused by Turks of sheltering a runaway slave, tortured, and eventually ransomed. He established a hermitage on the island of Evia which attracted a number of disciples. (TN)

5 A personification of death. In Greek mythology, Charos manned the boat that crossed the river Styx to deliver souls to Hades. Of course, the Saint's mother was not a pagan but in many Greek folk songs and stories the use of Charos as a personification of death persists. This is not a return to a worship of false deities but an artistic device. (TN)

Origin & Childhood Years

Let us allow the Elder himself to explain his family life in Asia Minor and later in Greece.

As a small child the Elder was sickly and sensitive. He was also very modest. The Elder would say, "My mother, because of my sickly constitution, called me a little autumnal bird." He continues:

> As a little two-year-old child my mother wrapped me up in her skirt and with my grandmother and my two young siblings we got on the boat for Greece. My father remained in Asia Minor, imprisoned by the Turks. One of the things I remember from my childhood is that when we got off at the port of Piraeus, I heard someone for the first time in my life say something blasphemous. Then my grandmother said, "Where have we come to? It would have been better to stay where we were and get slaughtered by the Turks than hear such words." In Asia Minor we didn't know this kind of sin: blasphemy.

From Piraeus the refugees were moved to different places in Greece. The Elder's family lived for two years in a warehouse together with other immigrant families in the village of Agios Georgios, Amfissa. During those two years they had no knowledge of their father's whereabouts. However, God's providence brought their father to the village where his family was living, and he found work with a housebuilder because he had previously worked in construction.

> My grandmother was passing by a building that was under construction and she heard my father's voice from inside, recognizing it immediately. This is the miraculous way that we were reunited with my father, full of emotion and indescribable joy. It was especially miraculous because my father thought

that we had all been killed and was even thinking about getting remarried, but God stopped it in this extraordinary manner.

During the following years, the family moved to Evia and established themselves in the village of Farakla, at the northern part of the island where they were given land upon which they built a house. This is the house that the Elder lived in until he was 30 years old. The Elder would reflect with emotion on the blessed and peaceful family life of his childhood years. His father was often away from the house working as a builder, therefore, his blessed mother Theodora was the Elder's main instructor.

> As a child I didn't have groups of friends. I rarely left the house: only for school, specific errands, and work. My mother was very attentive to the subject of modesty in her children. One time she saw me put my hands between my legs to keep them warm. To protect me from the invitation to sin and stirring of the body she told me discreetly and meekly: "Iakovos, my child, don't put your hands between your legs again because when children do this, their parents get tuberculosis and die."

> When I told her that my hands were cold and that I was putting them there to keep them warm, she knitted two woolen gloves, like woolen socks, which I could wear on my hands to keep them warm. My mother guided me with much discernment and caution on the topic of modesty. She had this wisdom and discernment from God which is why she herself lived modestly and ascetically. After the birth of her children, my parents did not come together again but they lived a spiritual life together as brother and sister. One of them slept on one side of the room,

the other on the other side, and the children slept in the middle of the room, all of them together on a straw mattress in front of the fireplace. It was a humble, blessed, holy, and ascetic life.

My mother taught me how to do prostrations, full prostrations, which is how I became accustomed to do many prostrations while praying. I stayed in the house and helped her with different work that housewives normally do. I loved her and it made me sad how tired she became. From my childhood I learned how to sew, how to make beds, and in general how to do all the household chores normally done by the women. This has greatly helped me as a monastic because I didn't have any difficulty in taking care of these types of chores.

When we lit the fireplace in the winter months my parents sat on one side of the fireplace; they each had their designated spots. We had so much respect for our mother and father. Even when they were not there, we never sat in their places, but we sat somewhere else—that is how much we respected them.

Every two weeks or so, a priest would come to serve the Divine Liturgy in our village because at that time there was no dedicated priest. When he came, I would go to the church from the night before to help serve in the altar; and when I got older, I chanted. Until everyone got to church, I would do full prostrations continuously. One time the priest remarked to me, "Iakovos my child, don't do prostrations on Sundays." I replied, "Father, I do prostrations because that is what my mother taught me to do."

> We had not been instructed much in confession but we would fast very strictly to prepare to commune. When it was time for us to receive Holy Communion we would kiss the hands of our parents and elders and then we would go to receive. Our restraint with regard to food to support acts of almsgiving was incredible, especially from my mother. We got by for a whole week with just 125 ounces of oil. It was not because we did not have the means. We had good income from our fields and my father was a builder—we could have had a wealthier lifestyle. But my mother had developed the divine virtue of almsgiving, and her hand was always open to the suffering and the poor—of which there were plenty in those years. We helped them with food as well as with clothing. She had such a merciful and giving soul she would give away even our basic necessities. It got to the point where my father and I would return from working (because I would help him at work as I got older) and we would not even have undergarments to change into because my mother had given them away. We had to just change into whatever clean pants we could find. But the grace of God was so rich: it warmed us and made us joyful, and everything was peaceful in our house.

In this sanctified environment the grace of God began to enlighten and direct the Elder.

> It used to bring me peace to go to funerals even if I did not have a reason to go. Other times I would spend time in the cemetery of the village, even when there was nothing going on, because I was melancholy or had some inner disturbance. I would go and think about the vanity and fleeting nature of

life and the remembrance of death began to live in my soul.

Illumined by the Holy Spirit which found the Elder's soul a pure vessel, he began to think about dedicating his life to God and becoming an ascetic when he grew up.

> That's what made me happy, to leave the house and go outside of the village into the surrounding hills where I found small caves (or some I dug myself). I would cover them with branches from the shrubs nearby and lay a small quilt over them. Then I would kneel inside the caves and I would pray for hours, imagining I was an ascetic.

Thus, we can see how the results of his familial, ascetic tradition began to present themselves. At the same time, the Elder's future was starting to become apparent. The prayers offered by his family at the celestial altar—from the hieromonks in Upper Jerusalem, from the hierarch, and principally from the saint that came from his family—began to produce fruits, enlightening, warming, and enriching the receptive soul of the Elder.

After the Elder completed elementary school, the teacher of the village encouraged the Elder's parents to send him to Chalkida for further schooling because of his intelligence and perfect performance in class. "But my parents," the Elder said, "preferred to keep me close to them, fearing that I would somehow be in danger far from the family." For the teacher, it seemed like a shame that the Elder wouldn't continue his education, because of his intelligence.

The Elder completed only elementary school, so that he would be taken up by the One who teaches unwritten wisdom—the true wisdom, by the One who turned fishermen into theologians, in order to show him how to be a true theologian and Father of the Church.

The great gift of faith and the humility of the Elder, as well as the prayers of his venerable mother, were the reasons for this marvelous, living relationship Fr. Iakovos had with Panagia and with all the saints. In this way, very simply, very naturally, heaven descended to earth. Truly, great are the accomplishments of faith!

> One time, when I was a small child, I suffered from such a bad cold that I fell in bed with difficulty breathing, with an extreme pain on the left side of my chest. There was no doctor in the village and our only refuge was God and His saints. In our house we had a small icon of St. Haralambos that worked miracles. It was a family heirloom from Asia Minor, very old, and made of silver. My mother prayed fervently and did many prostrations asking the saint for assistance.
>
> While I was lying in bed, I saw the hand of a priest, only from the wrist down, passing over my head and down to my chest in the spot where I had pain. He gently touched the spot and made the sign of the Cross over it. Immediately, the pain passed together with my difficulty breathing and I became well. I said to my mother, "Mother, I saw the hand of a priest sign me with the Cross and touch me and I am better; everything passed. His wrist even had some hair on it; that is how clearly I saw it." My mother replied, "My child, that was St. Haralambos that came and healed you. This day you must always remember and honor (it was the feast of the holy Apostle Thomas when the miracle happened), because you were dead and now you rose."
>
> Another time, again as a small child, I suffered from such a severe rash on the soles of my feet that these

huge wounds opened up, like deep cuts with water running out and it resulted in terrible pain. My feet could not be healed by all the normal treatments that they tried at that time, using lotions and balms made from wax and oil. My feet were like this for a long time and continued to get worse. I couldn't walk, or naturally, even wear shoes. I walked carefully around the house in considerable pain, with ointments on my feet and little pieces of paper stuck on top of the lesions. In this way my life became a martyrdom. I was so weak from this affliction with my feet, my mother had become anxious and she told me one day, "My child, I am disgusted by you with those feet."

Those words made me worried; they wounded me. Not because my mother was actually disgusted with me—would that even be possible? —but because of her extreme sorrow for my situation.

Around that time they brought a miracle-working icon of Panagia Xenias to Evia, and some faithful would bring the icon from village to village for the people to venerate it. We heard that the icon of the Panagia was in a neighboring village about two hours away by foot. There were a good number of villagers and children that decided to go and venerate her. I asked my mother to allow me to go as well. But she told me:

> Where are you going to walk my child with your feet the way they are now, especially so far? You won't be able to keep up with the others and you will get left behind all alone and could fall into danger. The foxes could eat you on the road.

She told me this so I would get scared and not want to go anymore. It just so happened that a priest who had come to our village to serve Divine Liturgy passed by the house. He overheard our conversation and said to my mother, "Theodora, let the child go. He wants to go so badly—don't stop him." My mother answered:

> Most reverend father (that is how the people of Asia Minor were accustomed to addressing priests), the child has a problem with his feet, that is why I'm keeping him back. Because you said that he should go, well, then he'll go.

My mother was embarrassed to argue with a priest, so she gave me permission to go like the humble and obedient soul that she was. The group of people had already begun their journey to the neighboring village. After only a few meters of walking barefoot (because I couldn't wear shoes), all the little papers covering my sores had fallen off and little stones, wood chips, and thorns were sticking to my feet because of the ointments. After a little while the lesions were full of debris and the pain that came was unbearable. Every step was a martyrdom. But that is how much yearning I had for Panagia. Because of my faith in her grace, I continued my journey like a martyr. Eventually we caught up with the miracle-working icon on the road to the village toward which it was headed. I ran, limping with terrible pains, and venerated our Panagia and asked her to heal me, to save me from this martyrdom of my feet. I spoke to her like a child to its mother, and with pain I remember saying:

> O my Panagia, my mother told me that she was fed up with me because of my feet. But you are not disgusted with me. I beg you, make me well so that I can walk like the other children.

I stood crying in the street, stroking her holy icon and then rubbing my torn up feet which were full of dirt, caked with mud from the water that was running from the lesions. As we arrived in the village, they proceeded to put the icon of Panagia on top of a chair in the church and the people came and venerated it. One by one they returned to their homes as the sun set, but I stayed for a little while alone in the church. It was already getting dark, and it would take about two hours to get home. I stayed by myself with Panagia, and when I saw that there was no one else around, I told her:

> My Panagia, now that we're alone, please make me well. Please heal my feet and I won't be ungrateful, I will work when I get older and I will do whatever I can to repay your grace.

While saying these things, I was crying and stroking the holy icon and then my swollen feet. After I implored her, I went outside of the church. I could not believe it, but my feet didn't hurt at all and I was able to walk easily. I went a little bit further before spitting a little in my hand and cleaning off the sole of one foot and then the other. *Great is your grace lady Theotokos!* No lesions, no open wounds—only white scars like little marks in the areas where just a little while ago there had been those massive cuts. It was like many years had passed and only the memory of my illness remained. I turned around immediately and, with tears of joy streaming down my face, I

> thanked our Panagia. Then I resumed my trip and ran back to my village light as a bird—on the same road that just a little while ago I had walked on with so much struggle.

The holy father had an especially great love for the small chapels and shrines[6] of the saints that the piety of Christians had sowed like seeds in every corner of the Greek countryside. From his young childhood he would go to all the little chapels, lighting the oil lamps, sweeping them, and praying there by himself in the quiet of the countryside. The Elder would say:

> I really enjoyed seeing the vigil lamp lit in the middle of the night. I would sit there and look at the flickering light, feeling happy and comforted.

The Elder would also counsel:

> When you see a small chapel or shrine you should always make your Cross as you pass by and call upon the saint, because the saints are present there and their grace helps us.

The Elder was especially fond of a small chapel dedicated to St. Paraskevi that sat on a hill outside a village. When he was younger he would go there often and pray to the saint.

> I dug out little steps in the dirt with my hands on the path going up to the chapel so that it would be easier for pilgrims to visit. I cut down a bush and used it to sweep the church. I lit the oil lamps and I would sit and gaze at the icons in complete silence on top

---

[6] It is customary in Greece for those who are especially devoted to a particular saint to erect a small chapel with an icon of the saint, a censer, and a vigil lamp. (TN)

of the deserted hill. I was not afraid of being there alone and I never had the temptation to be fearful.

I saw the saint dressed as a nun coming out of the holy altar, going through her church, going outside and then crouching down and cleaning the vigil lamps. With my childish mind I thought she was cleaning her dishes just like my mother did every evening. No matter how tired my mother was she always washed the dishes, saying, "Heaven forbid I would die in the middle of the night and the other women would find all my dirty dishes and be scandalized." So that is how I understood the situation; I thought that St. Paraskevi was washing her dishes.

One evening, I went as usual to the chapel and a few meters away I saw the saint standing there and she said to me: "Come here Iakovos, let me talk to you."

I was scared and my feet were shaking.

"I'm afraid to come close to you. Tell me what you want from over there where you're standing. I'm afraid to come."

Then the saint spoke to me, saying, "Why are you scared of me? You have come here so many times. You look after my church and light my vigil lamps. I want to tell you many things. Ask me what favor you want from me. What gift should I give you?"

Then I told her, "Let me ask my mother first and then I'll tell you."

I returned running to the village for my house. I told my mother that I had seen St. Paraskevi and she asked me what favor I would like her to do for me.

> My mother asked me, "You saw St. Paraskevi? How did you see her? What happened exactly?"
>
> So, I explained the details of what had occurred, and my mother told me, "My child, go ask St. Paraskevi to tell you your future."
>
> The next night I went to the small chapel, and I saw the saint again waiting for me outside of the church dressed as a nun. I stood a little bit away from her and said, "I would like you to tell me my future."
>
> Then the saint said, "Your fortune in your life will be that much gold will pass through your hands," and the saint made a big gesture to show great abundance, "but it won't touch you."
>
> And in fact, immeasurable amounts of money did pass through my hands but it all went to good use—to the suffering, to the poor, to those who had need. St. Paraskevi told me many other things and then I ran back home.

The villagers, seeing the holy life that little Iakovos lived, respected him and thought of him as a child of the Church, as a child of God.

> Because there was no priest in the village, many times different people would ask me to read a prayer for their various needs, especially for sicknesses, believing that they would be helped.

Listen to the Elder describe a few more events from his childhood:

THE FAINTING GIRL

One day I was sitting at my house as I usually do, looking out the window, and I saw a girl about 12 years old pass by, but she looked much older than her age. An elderly woman sitting on the other side of the road remarked when she saw her, "Oh bravo, girl, you could be 18!"[7]

Immediately the girl fell down unconscious, obviously a case of demonic attack. They took her to her house where she was very close to dying. In the middle of their distress the poor people, not having a doctor or a priest, thought about little Iakovos. Her brother came to our house and begged me to go and read a prayer for her so that his sister would not die.

I told him, "I am not a priest or a doctor. I'm not coming."

He grabbed me by the hand and pulled me, saying, "You are a child of God! God listens to you! Come and read a prayer so that my sister doesn't die." I replied, "You go ahead and then I'll follow."

"No way," the boy said, "You're coming with me now because if I leave you will go and hide somewhere."

What was I supposed to do? When I got to the house I saw the girl lying down with her eyes turned up,

---

[7] The Elder likely relates this detail to connect the illness that follows with the folk superstition of the 'evil-eye.' Misfortune and evil are associated with receiving compliments. The Elder is not necessarily promoting this folk belief but as a small child he is relating to us the way he saw the world. In one sense we should also be careful when paying compliments to others in that it might bring about feelings of pride which can lead to later falls. (TN)

breathing heavily in a terrible state. Then I told them, "Say a prayer so that God makes her better."

I said the "Our Father" and whatever other prayers I knew. I asked them for holy water and sprinkled some on her and immediately she got up, miraculously healthy. I left the house quickly to avoid any praises or thanks because God performs miracles, not men. A little while later the girl's brother came to our house with chickpeas, beans, and the like to thank me for healing his sister. I didn't keep any of it because, if I kept these gifts, the next time God would not hear my prayers.

A Woman in Labor

One time, a woman was not able to give birth and was having a difficult labor. Again, they forced me to go to her house right when she was ready to have the baby. I went into the other room and read prayers and in a little while the woman gave birth.

The Epidemic

Another time there was a mumps epidemic. Mothers would bring their children to my house swollen and feverish so that I could read prayers for them. One of the children, even though he was sick, began to laugh and teased me, saying:

"What, you mean Iakovos is going to read a prayer and I am going to get better?"

The next day all of the other children had returned to normal, but only that one child got worse. He had swollen up even more and it was very serious. His mother brought him back to our house crying and she begged me to pray for her son. Then I told her, "Tell your son to repent and to not laugh during the prayer or to make fun of it unless he wants to die."

The boy repented and I read the prayer over him. The next day he was healed.

The Demoniac Woman

We had a woman in our village who was possessed by a demon. She came to our house and asked me to read a prayer for her. She grabbed me by the hand. So I took holy water and we went to the church where I read a prayer for her. Outside of the church the demon could be seen fearsome and threatening. The poor woman told me that she saw the sharp, white, glistening tooth of a dragon jammed into the keyhole of the door threatening her. But she spoke to the demon and said,

> "Because Iakovos is reading a prayer for me I am not afraid of you!"

I sprinkled her with holy water and she was healed.

The Elder often spoke about the ascetic lifestyle of his family, especially their virtue of fasting.

> When it was Great Lent we fasted very strictly. Even with all the difficult physical labor that we had to do we waited until the Annunciation and Palm Sunday to eat a little fried cod or a few fresh sardines, which were as delicious as candy. These were the only fish that we got in the village (and these only rarely). My mother tested me to see if I was really fasting, with my heart, and she told me one time during Lent:

> "Iakovos my child, you are so skinny, why don't you eat an egg?"
>
> "Mama, if I eat an egg now I won't truly experience the Resurrection. I want to eat a Paschal egg so that I can really appreciate Pascha."

> When Great Lent was over and Pascha arrived, after the Resurrection service, I didn't eat my egg immediately, but I took it and travelled outside of the village to the outskirts of town in the fields. There I would chant "Christ is Risen!" and the other hymns of the feast with all the strength of my soul, with yearning, and with compunction until the afternoon. Then I would sit down and eat the egg. It didn't smell like a normal egg; it had a sweet fragrance.

The Elder spoke about his life as he was beginning to work.

> After finishing primary school, I began to follow my father to work in construction, sometimes in our village and sometimes in other villages. I worked with him side-by-side. Sometimes I would carry stones and large cornerstones. With a lot of effort, I made the plaster mud and whatever else needed to be done. When it was a fasting period or Wednesday or Friday, I preferred not to eat the food that was offered to us by the people for whom we were building. If I found a few olives I would eat them off to the side. This was something that after many years I was reminded of, when people would come visit the monastery and relate incidents to me from my own childhood.

> How true it is that an example teaches us. What a permanent impression an example leaves on souls in contrast to words! If the food happened to be tasty, I preferred to return to my home village instead of staying there and enjoying the food. The next day I would return to work even though it was far away.
>
> Of course, I walked so fast that it seemed as if I were flying. Nothing ever bothered me on the road. I would light the vigil lamps at the little shrines and chapels along the road and, before I knew it, I was at my house.
>
> At some points along the road, I would see a demon. One time I remember I said to my father, "Father, do you see that evil thing?" And I would point it out to him.
>
> He didn't see anything, but I saw a demon: all black and with big eyes, rolling and red like a flame.

The Elder explained that some mountainous areas were dwelling places of unclean spirits.

> On the road, there was a spot that I passed on my way home from work while I was riding on a donkey. The animal would stop and snort like he was terrified and stamp his feet. He wouldn't move forward because there was a demon lying in the middle of the road who was trying to pull me off the donkey and hurt me. I would pray, make the sign of the Cross, and call upon St. George for help because close by was a small chapel dedicated to him. Then the donkey would jump very high as if it was going over a hurdle and it would pass by this one point on the road (with great danger to it and myself). God

really protected me and kept me on the saddle and I wasn't killed. It was a miracle.

Eventually the Elder's mother passed on from this temporary life to eternal life.

The years passed and I reached the age of 18. One day my mother called for me and said:

"Iakovos my child, after 3 days I will be leaving."

Then I asked her, "What do you mean mother? You're going? Where are you leaving?"

"My child, after three days I will leave, I will die. My Angel came and told me so."

"Mother, you saw your Angel? What was he like? How did you see him? What did he tell you?" I asked her.

"My child, I saw him—don't ask me what he was like. He came and told me: *Theodora, after three days when the sun is rising in the east like a reed I will come and take you. Take care to be ready.*"

I was so upset. It is easy for someone to understand how upsetting this was if one considered the bond between a mother and child: a physical and an emotional bond, but for me it was our spiritual bond, in the soul. Almost immediately my mother fell very ill, probably with pneumonia. It was a Monday. On Wednesday, after three days, as the Angel had foretold, she got up with a lot of effort. She put on the one change of clothes she had (she had given away the rest as charity), and she laid down on a sheet looking towards the east. The sun rose to the height of a reed and then she called out for me, embraced me, and gave me her blessing, saying:

> My child, you will become a priest and your siblings will kiss your hands. You will become what you were destined to be, but I will leave you with one burden: your sister. Protect her, raise her, and after that you can go to fulfill your destiny with my blessing.

She said this, took three quiet breaths, and fell asleep. Truly a venerable death.

I passed out from my pain and grief. I went to the cemetery and cried so much at my mother's grave that I passed out again from sorrow. I said:

> "God is punishing me by taking my mother, and I will never go to church again."

But one night my mother appeared to me in my sleep and said:

> "Iakovos, my child, you come to the cemetery and cry at my tombstone. Do you think with those tears of yours you are making my dress wet? God didn't punish you by taking me. My time came and God took me. And that thing you said about not going to church again, don't say that. Go just like you used to."

From this experience I was comforted, and I was obedient to her holy words. I continued the same holy ascetical life until I was 27 years old when I began my military service.

Ὁ π. Ἰάκωβος Στρατιώτης τό 1949 μέ τό Συνταγματάρχη του Πολύκαρπο Ζώη καί συναδέλφους του.

Father Iakovos as a soldier in 1949, together with his colonel Polycarp Zoe and his fellow soldiers.

CHAPTER 2

The Elder's Life in the Military

The years when the Elder did his military service were some of the worst years for our homeland. It was the period of the civil war, or rather the war of brothers murdering brothers.

The humble, guileless, and peaceful Elder trained in the military then became a military officer in the city of Volos. With his typical, pure humor he explained some of the events of his training:

Portrait of the Elder in the Military.

> I was sitting in class, learning about weapons theory, looking very attentively. My mind, though, was in my village, occupied with prayer, as if I was back in the churches and chapels there. One time there was a particularly gruff and barbaric instructor who caught me a little distracted and angrily hit me on the head with his gun. I meekly replied and complained that he hit me. God didn't let him go

unpunished, however. Almost immediately, a big gust of wind blew a large thorn into his eye. It hurt him so badly that he was in danger of losing his sight. He was terrified and thought that I had cursed him somehow. Naturally, I didn't curse him but God afflicted him in this way to soften his hardened heart.

St. Haralambos continued to protect the Elder during his military service.

> While I was serving with the military, I always kept with me the miraculous icon of St. Haralambos. I frequently implored the saint to keep me from having to serve in the armed regiment, because I was not a man for blood. When the commander of the regiment was picking which soldiers would serve in the armed fighting unit, I held on tightly to the icon of the saint and begged him to not allow the commander to see me and choose me to be among the fighters. Naturally the saint always "blinded" the commander and he never selected me for this.
>
> One time I was a scout in the area of Pilio and I was assigned to watch for any signs of movement. I sat in front of the machine gun and I took out the icon of St. Haralambos. I placed it on top of the gun and told the saint, "Okay, my saint, you keep watch like a scout. Keep an eye over my area from here to there." I showed him the area under my direction and, without a care in the world, I began to pray.
>
> Truly the grace of St. Haralambos was there. One time a group of *antartes*[8] was hidden among a herd of sheep. I was in grave danger. One of them thought about sneaking up from behind and killing me.

---

8   The Greek guerrilla fighters fighting against the Greek state. (TN)

> But the saint touched the heart of one of the other fighters, who stopped him from killing me, saying, "Leave the kid alone, what did he do to us? Plus, we shouldn't put ourselves in danger without a serious reason."
>
> Thus, I was saved by the intercessions of the saint. I didn't even know about the danger that I survived until a shepherd came by the next day and told me about it.

The Elder continued to seek out opportunities to attend church.

> One day I asked for leave and went to the small chapel of Panagia, the Annunciation in New Ionia, Volos. Outside stood two priests. I made the sign of the Cross and kissed their hands. I heard them then remark, "There you go—a pious soldier."
>
> The other turned to me and said, "Soldier—Fr. Aimilianos in the village of St. George of Amfissa, do you know him?"
>
> "I'm related to him," I replied.
>
> Then the priest, full of emotion, said to me, "My child, I could tell by your face. You look so much like Fr. Aimilianos, I knew it."
>
> Fr. Aimilianos was the only married priest in our extended family; all the rest were hieromonks. He and his *presvytera*, Aimilia, were so virtuous and holy that his name was well known in the area he served.

From Volos, the Elder was transferred to Athens. It was there that God enlightened the heart of the Elder's commanding officer, the blessed Polycarpos Zoe, and he took the young Iakovos in like his own child.

> Every day he would give me written permission to go to church. That was how, during my time serving there, I was able to visit and venerate almost all of the churches in Athens and Piraeus.

His commanding officer had so much respect and love for the Elder that, even after the Holy Elder had left for the monastery of St. David, he frequently visited him. He even donated the funds necessary to build a chapel to St. Polycarpos, the Bishop of Smyrna, outside of the monastery.

> After Polycarpos' repose and then after his relics were exhumed,[9] I kept the bones of his right hand at the monastery—the hand that wrote all the permissions that allowed me to go to church. I always commemorated him together with my parents.

Of course, the Elder could not completely escape the trials of life as a soldier, especially from his fellow soldiers. They were motivated by the devil to tease the Elder, to make fun of him, to jokingly call him "the priest," and they mocked him using the typical jokes of the military. They could never explain or understand with their secular minds the strange and "unnatural" conduct of the Elder. For all the efforts the Elder made to hide his life in Christ, the other soldiers never missed an opportunity to note with detail his godly behavior.

> When I was in the barracks, I would cover myself with a blanket, make my Cross secretly, and say prayers. Suddenly, the person sleeping next to me,

---

9 It is a common practice in Greece that after three years the body of a reposed person is exhumed and the bones are cleaned for storage in an ossuary. (TN)

or probably below me, because we were sleeping in bunk beds, yelled at me:

"Iakovos—why are you moving, why do you keep wriggling around?"

"Oh, nothing. Nothing," I said.

"No—you're making your Cross again; you're praying again! I mean come on, we just said prayers all together. Why are you keeping on by yourself?"

"I'm not doing anything wrong," I replied. "I am just saying prayers."

One time I went on an outing with some of my comrades to Piraeus, and they said:

"Come here Iakovos so we can show you something."

I was completely unsuspecting and followed them. They brought me to a particular spot and said, "Look here."

I looked down some stairs through an entrance to a basement and I saw people dancing naked.

"Why did you bring me here?" I asked them.

One of them, tempted by the devil, grabbed me from behind and tried to drag me downstairs.

"Come on let's go down there!"

Then the meek Iakovos, full of divine zeal, seized his comrade and threatened him to never take him on a walk again. Like another Joseph, he fled from sin.

The virtuous life always teaches and shows fruits after years. I mean, if I went with them and joined them in their "activities" and continued with them, what good could have come from it?

In this way the Elder passed these three years of military service in a blessed way. He was 30 years old when he returned to his village and finished raising his little sister, keeping his promise to his mother. Then he was free to follow what his heart desired most from childhood: the monastic life.

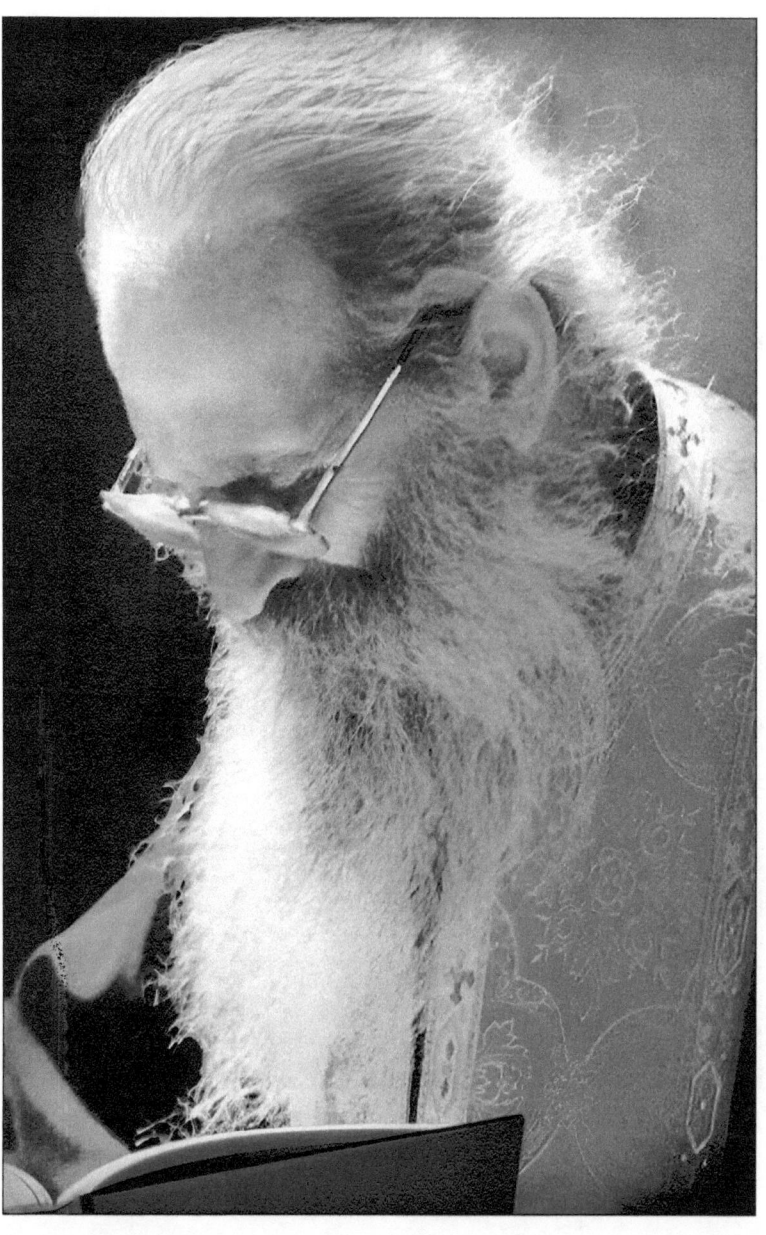

The Eldress Makrina and sisters of the Monastery of the Odygetria in Volos together with St. Iakovos.

CHAPTER 3
The Monastic Life of the Elder

The saint's desire for the monastic way of life turned towards the life of the desert, specifically towards the Holy Lands.

> I wanted to visit the Holy Lands which had sanctified my forefathers (Ed. —At a later point we will discuss the holy life of his ancestor who was a hieromonk at the Holy Sepulcher). I wanted to find a cave, to be fed on only the wild plants that grew there, and drink whatever water was there—by myself, unknown to the world, and to pass the rest of my life in prayer, worshipping God.
>
> Before I set off for the Holy Lands with these thoughts in my heart, I thought it was necessary to go to the monastery of St. David to ask for the blessing and the intercessions of the saint. After a very long, multiple hour hike through the mountains, following only foot paths (there was no road at that time), I arrived at the monastery.
>
> As soon as I turned the corner, all of a sudden, I saw a change, something completely different from the wild land around me. It was beautiful, majestic, and from a different time. Looking around, I saw

it transform into the most beautiful space—with small houses like little palaces suspended in the air, scattered around the monastery, so that it all had the appearance of being a small, awe-inspiring community. It reminded me of how Kallithea[10] appeared during that time.

Outside of the monastery I saw an old, venerable looking monk waiting with white hair and a white beard—it was St. David himself, whom I addressed saying:

> "Elder, what a beautiful place this is! What beautiful little houses these are! Where have I come? I've never seen this before!"

> Then the saint responded to me saying, "This is the city of the ascetics. Each one has his own house."

Totally captivated by the heavenly vision, I spoke to him imploringly:

> "Elder, is it possible to give me a house like this? I want one more than anything."

> The saint said to me, "My child, if you were going to stay here, we would have given you one. But you came here just to venerate and then leave."

> Spontaneously I blurted out, "Elder, I will stay."

As soon as I gave him my pledge, it appeared as if the wall of the monastery opened and the saint passed through it before it closed. I lost him before my eyes.

---

10 A large suburb of Athens. (TN)

Suddenly, everything else disappeared.

Where there had been the "city of ascetics," the land returned to the way it was: a wild cliff and an unkempt, overgrown forest. It was all in ruins with only two or three cells ready to collapse with roofs caving in. The 'main church' was small and neglected and looked more like a chapel than the main church of a monastery.

Without waiting, because I gave my promise to the saint, I came as a simple pilgrim and found myself as a brother of the monastery. I made a prostration and gave a pledge to the saint that I would serve him with all my heart. At the monastery, at that time there lived two or three older monks according to the idiorrhythmic way. Each of them had his own cell, kitchen, and food. They cooked alone, ate alone, and did their work alone. The abbot of the monastery, the ever-memorable Archimandrite Nikodemos, was appointed by the Metropolitan of Chalkida. He lived in Limni and served there as a priest. He came to the monastery every so often. When he came, he stayed for only a little while and then would return to his parish in Limni.

About his own Elder, the abbot Fr. Nikodemos, Elder Iakovos always said that he was a virtuous man, ethical, and very merciful. He endured difficulties in his life because he had diabetes, but especially because he was persecuted by his fellow man, unfortunately within the Church. So, persecuted and driven out from where he lived, the place where he served the Lord, he gave his soul into the hands of God, who said: "Blessed are those who are persecuted for righteousness' sake."[11]

---

11 Matthew 5:10.

> Beginning my monastic life without having an abbot or my spiritual father in the monastery, essentially alone, I put obedience first as an inviolable principle. Obedience is the base and foundation of monastic life. I didn't do anything without a blessing, without the permission of the abbot. I asked for his blessing for everything. This was not easy because it required many difficult journeys, four to five hours on foot, to go down to Limni to get his blessing for the different things in my personal life or for the monastery.

However, a miraculous event took place within a few days of the Elder joining the monastery.

> By my nature, I didn't have any facial hair, only a few sparse wisps of hair. I was clean shaven. But it seemed to me that a monk should be venerable and respectable with a full beard and mustache. I asked Panagia and St. David for help to grow a beard.

Miraculously, within one week a full beard and mustache began to grow which he kept until the end of his life.

> That is how, from the beginning, I loved the saint with all my heart; St. David is a great saint. A divine zeal was established in my heart and I worked with my body and soul for the saint, for the glory of God. I kept the cycle of services of the monastery, and during the remaining hours of the day, I worked tirelessly inside and outside. The monastery was in ruins and had been in disrepair for years.
>
> It was very rare for pilgrims to visit. Only for the feast day of the monastery, once a year, some people from the surrounding villages would arrive. I busied myself with various crafts to restore the dilapidated buildings of the monastery.

I built, did the carpentry, and labored to restore some rooms which could be used to house pilgrims. Outside of the monastery I cultivated the untamed land. I dug up weeds and shrubs, working very hard, until everything was cleaned up. Then I planted beans, lentils, chickpeas, and other things so that we could have food for the monastery as well as provide charity to the poor people that lived nearby. Poverty at that time was the norm.

At the beginning, the devil incited the other fathers of the monastery that were living an idiorrhythmic life. Instead of being happy that this new man—so obedient and full of love, zeal, and humility—had arrived, they revolted and did what they could to snuff his zeal and frustrate him so that he would leave the monastery. These fathers persecuted the Elder so much during the first steps of his monastic life that we will not record the specific events the Elder explained to us, so that we do not condemn anyone instead of offering something beneficial.

On account of the snake's devious counsel, the blameless Elder became to his fellow ascetics one who was a burden even to look upon.[12] But what is stronger than faith, humility, and love? These were virtues that the Elder had which he confessed with unbelievable humility, glorifying God who had granted them to him. During the trial of the incredible poverty of the monastery, the Elder undertook the virtue of fasting to such a degree that he not only fasted from foods, but also drank water sparingly. The Lord granted him such continence that he only drank water on the weekends. Within his soul there flowed a stream, "a fountain of water springing up into everlasting life,"[13] and drinking water was

---

12 "He has become for us as a refutation of our purposes; even seeing him is a burden to us." Wisdom of Solomon 2:14.

13 John 4:14.

no longer necessary. Christ became his food, his clothing, his rejoicing, and his gladness; and in this way, his physical needs were satiated and he no longer needed material nourishment.

His cell was no more than a ruined shack without glass in the windows, with old shutters that didn't close well. During the heavy winter, when the snow was meters high and the cold intolerable, the Elder lit a small fire inside his frozen cell. The wind would blow snow into his room through the slits of the shutters and create a white path on the floor of the cell.

> I took the Psalter with the long candle we would use to light the *polyeleos*,[14] and I chanted verses all night until I made my way through the entire Psalter. That is how I kept warm with the flame that warmed the ascetics, the hermits, and the stylites. I had a lot: I had tiles above my head—the stylites had nothing. If I was in a cave like a hermit I wouldn't have the comforts of a cell, even if it was in disrepair. These are the types of thoughts that brought me comfort.

> One time during a very difficult winter, when the snow in the courtyard had frozen over, I went down very carefully to church for the service. Just before I entered the church I slipped and fell very hard on my spine, right above my hip. I must have fractured some of the vertebrae because I got up with extreme pain before I managed to make it back to my cell. I laid down on the old door of the cell that I used as a bed in extreme pain, without moving.

> It wasn't that I couldn't stand up; I couldn't even make the slightest movement. I was stuck there lying

---

14 The large chandelier with candles that is in the center of the nave of the church suspended under the dome. (TN)

down, alone, frozen, hungry, and thirsty—not for one or two days but for 14 days. During this time not one of the other fathers came and opened the door of my cell to see if I was alive or dead or to offer me any help. I spent two weeks like this and begged St. David, saying:

> "My saint, I came here for you. You see that I can't take anymore; please, I beg you, please come and help me, come heal me. But don't come here as yourself, because I'm a cowardly man and I can't bear to see you. But come as one of the brothers of the monastery."

As soon as I finished this prayer, the door opened and the saint came in the appearance of one of the brothers of the monastery. He said to me:

"What's wrong Fr. Iakovos?"

"I fell and I'm in terrible pain. I've been stuck here for two weeks lying down."

Then the saint said to me, "Who am I? Am I Father *so and so*?"

I was hesitant to say that he was St. David, so I told him, "Yes, you are Father *so and so*."

The saint then said to me, "Come on let me help you. Sit up and show me where it hurts."

I told him then, "If I could sit, I would get up and sit. But I can't move."

"Come on. I'll help you," the saint said.

And then I sat up with his help. The saint stood behind me back-to-back and helped me stay upright.

I felt that his back was priestly—that is, I could feel the grace of the priesthood. Then the saint made the sign of the Cross over the areas where I was in pain and over my hips and my neck and head. Everything passed immediately: no more pain, not a trace of injury, only joy and happiness. Immediately the saint opened the door and went outside. Then I began to feel sorry for myself and my cowardice because I didn't even make a prostration to thank him.

God frequently lets His athletes get to the point where they've reached the bitter end of their physical and spiritual endurance, and when it seems as if there is no more human hope then He intervenes. Completely healthy, the Elder continued his asceticism with St. David as his assistant, his brother, and his protector (as he called the saint when he prayed to him). With every occurrence, the Elder would go to the icon of St. David and talk to him and ask for his help.

To show the lightness of his soul and its richness in Christ, as well as the love of the Father, we should mention one or two specific events.

There was a time the abbot, Fr. Nikodemos, sent a written order to give a specific amount of oil to one of the workers as a payment for work he had done at the monastery. The Elder took the letter from the abbot and went before the monastery's icon of St. David. There he read the letter and then gave the oil to the worker as he was required to do. As the worker was going down to Limni, he met with the abbot who happened to be going up to the monastery. In their conversation, Fr. Nikodemos realized that the worker had been paid in oil, but Fr. Nikodemos did not seem to remember he had asked Fr. Iakovos to do this. As soon as the abbot reached the monastery, Fr. Iakovos received him at the entrance. Fr. Nikodemos furiously grabbed Fr. Iakovos by the throat and threatened to choke him. He was upset that he had given away the oil because the monastery would be negatively impacted. Surprised, Fr. Iakovos told him:

> My Elder, as a young child I was saved from the Turks when we were driven out of Asia Minor, and I survived so many dangers because God protected me. But if you think that I should be strangled, then do as you think. I gave the oil to the man because I received your letter to do so and then I read it to St. David.

Then the abbot said to him, "Well, then where is the letter? Show me."

Fr. Iakovos ran to his cell and retrieved the letter, lit a candle, and began to burn it in the fireplace so that Fr. Nikodemos wouldn't see it and become bothered by his own behavior.

> The abbot came to the cell, out of breath, and saw the letter burning. The abbot said to him, "What papers are burning there?"
>
> Fr. Iakovos replied, "Oh nothing, my Elder. Just some old scraps. Please forgive me; you were right."
>
> Fr. Nikodemos began to soften, to chuckle, and then he departed from the cell quietly.
>
> The Elder explained later, "He either did it to test if I would argue for myself, or he actually forgot because of his blood sugar problems. God knows. But in any case, I wasn't sorry for burning the letter."

Another event transpired with one of the older fathers who never looked favorably upon the Elder. Fr. Iakovos would go to the father's cell and serve him with love. Fr. Iakovos would offer him his own food so the older father could be comfortable, even if Fr. Iakovos had to go hungry. But the other monk's heart had grown so hard from temptation by the devil that he didn't even say one kind word to Fr. Iakovos. Even on Pascha no one would eat together, everyone ate on their own.

> There was no way I could eat alone on such a big feast day. I found a worker and told him to stay at the monastery and at least eat a piece of bread with me. "Come on," I told him. "Let's eat together and crack a Paschal egg together."

That one brother who was hard-hearted to Fr. Iakovos had a tragic ending. He was going to light the heater in his room and his clothing caught fire. He was completely burned from head to foot and only lived a few days more in total agony. Fr. Iakovos cared for him during this time, tending to all his physical needs with a spirit of self-sacrifice. The monk's situation was dire and there was no medical help at that time. His life ended in extreme pain without getting his spiritual affairs in order.[15]

The devil saw that the Elder was coming out well-tested and better off because of these battles with others. So God allowed the Elder to be attacked more noticeably, in the way that other God-bearing fathers of the desert life experienced.

> I was working on repairing some of the rooms in the monastery. In the afternoon I got tired and decided to lie down for a little bit on a bed in one of the rooms where I was repairing the ceiling and the floor. All of a sudden, the door flew open, and something dressed like a soldier abruptly entered. He was wearing old pants and had only one eye

---

15 In another place we will relate how the Elder was made aware of the state of this monk's soul, as well as that of his own Elder, the abbot Fr. Nikodemos. (TN)

on his forehead. He said to me gruffly, "You're still here? Now you're going to suffer."

Then a swarm of 18 demons entered the room—some had the faces of people, while some looked like apes and other animals. They jumped on top of me and started to hit me and torment me. I tried to make my Cross, but three of them grabbed my arm and pinned it down before one of them pulled my fingers apart so that I couldn't form with my three fingers the sign of the Precious Cross. They beat me and tortured me in ways which I cannot describe. I was bleeding from my mouth and my nose. My lips were swollen, and my beard and hair were pulled out. My fingers were twisted, my shoulder was pulled out of its socket, and my ears were full of their hateful, ugly words. One of them said to me:

> "Do you see me? I'm the one who grabs you by the throat and doesn't let you read clearly." Another one, "I'm the one who does such and such."

Each one of them presented themselves to me and told me how they tempt or attack me. Finally, I was able to get my hand free and make my Cross, then they departed quickly out of the window, leaving me half-dead. I fixed my clothes as best as I could and went down the stairs to the kitchen. There was an older woman who was visiting the monastery as a pilgrim. As soon as she saw me, she was terrified and I told her, "You didn't come up and help me; the demons were trying to kill me."

The woman told me, "Fr. Iakovos, I heard the banging and the loud noise, but thought it was you working on something up there!"

These evil demons, who were so terrible and large, showed the power that the Lord gave to the Elder—to endure these attacks but also to become rich with grace.

> I tried to do my ascetical struggle in secret. I would wait until it was dark outside and the other fathers were in their cells. Then I would sneak out through the back door of the monastery and walk toward the ascetic cave of the saint. I couldn't see anything as I moved forward through the deep darkness. Whenever I would ask the saint for help, I would tell him, "You, my saint, my brother, help me to get to your cave."

> And then a star came down from the sky and seemed like it was on my forehead, illuminating the path in front of me so that I was able to see and reach the cave of the saint. Inside the holy elder (St. David) was there, alive, waiting for me. And he said to me, "Sit, rest."

> I would wait with great respect for the saint to leave the cave and then I would do my all-night prayer to the Lord. When the sun was about to rise, I would leave the cave and once again the little star would come down and illuminate the path so that I could return to the monastery. It was time for the morning service so I would go immediately to ring the bell. The fathers, not knowing that I was up all night, would say, "Oh Fr. Iakovos is awake," and then head down to the church.

The Elder relates his journey to the priesthood:

> One day the abbot came to the monastery and said to me, "Get cleaned up, wash yourself, and comb your hair; we're going down to Chalkida."

I didn't know why he wanted me to go with him, but I was obedient to his command. We went down to Chalkida to the Holy Metropolis. The metropolitan at that time was the blessed Gregory: a holy man, very priestly, poor, and a lover of monastics. He received us with fatherly affection. There they told me that the plan was that I would receive the great honor of the priesthood. Never in my life had I wanted positions or honors, nor did I imagine in my mind that I would be worthy of such an honor. I accepted it only out of obedience to my elder and respect for the holy bishop. So Metropolitan Gregory ordained me as a deacon and then a priest-monk. He gave me as a gift and keepsake a small icon of Panagia, saying, "Take this icon of Panagia, Fr. Iakovos, to protect you up in that wilderness where you live."

I have had that small icon on top of my bed for all these years. A few days later I also received written permission to be a spiritual father, so I was then able to confess the faithful.

Elder Iakovos processing with the Epitaphios on Holy Friday.

CHAPTER 4

The Priestly Life of the Elder

The Elder relates the details of the beginning of his priestly ministry:

> I began my priestly ministry in a monastery, following the *typikon* of the daily cycle of services and adding to it the celebration of the Divine Liturgy every day. Very early in the morning, we began the service and finished a little before dawn. I was able to partake daily of the Pure Mysteries and I felt such a power inside of me that I was like a lion. I had such a divine fire burning in my soul that all day I wasn't hungry or thirsty; nor did I feel hot or cold. From the morning until night, I worked without feeling tired. Even on the hot summer afternoons, when the other fathers would rest in their cells and cool off a bit, I would carry heavy dirt to the gardens I was cultivating outside of the monastery.
>
> One time the abbot Fr. Nikodemos came to the monastery, and seeing me working in the hot afternoon, said to me:
>
>> "Fr. Iakovos—you should go to your cell and rest. Don't work in the heat of the day."

And then to tease me he said, "I'm going to lock you in your cell to force you to rest."

I told him, "I'll jump out of the window."

The elder responded, "Oh really? If I locked you in there, you would jump out?"

"No, of course not," I said. "But I said it because I have so much zeal to work for the saint. I am not tired; the heat doesn't bother me, and I don't want to waste time resting."

At that time in the Metropolis there were not many priests, so I ended up serving the areas surrounding the monastery. For many years I offered my efforts to approximately 30 villages and towns in the surrounding area of the monastery. I would rotate through all the villages, providing for the general priestly needs of the people: baptisms, weddings, funerals, and more. The people of the surrounding area hadn't had a priest for many years, so they had not attended church, received Holy Communion, or gone for confession—they were like sheep without a shepherd.

The churches of the villages, and especially the countless chapels (which were a "weakness" of the Elder's) were completely run down. In addition to renovating the buildings of the monastery, the Elder's zeal extended to the temples of God with souls and without souls (that is, to the people and the houses of worship). It was like a fire that extended throughout the surrounding area, but not one that burned it up and left a desert in its wake, rather, one that warmed, enlightened, sheltered, and gave a new birth to everything and everyone.

> When I went to the monastery, the surrounding mountains and hills were bare because of the wildfires that had burned there before—only a few, sparse pines and firs had survived. Whenever I would go around doing different chores, I would keep seeds from pinecones in my pocket. I would scatter them all around the surrounding area, and little by little, with the saint's typical protection, and mostly through his prayers, the forest came back to life—the new trees took root, and the surrounding hills were overgrown with pine trees.

The Elder said special prayers to preserve the forest, especially from wildfires which are caused by the devil's spite, who tries to work through his instruments to destroy. The forest, among many things, was a source of economic support for the surrounding areas. Resin would be extracted and trees would be harvested for timber.

> In all seasons I would go on foot, or with a donkey if I knew ahead of time, to the village from Saturday afternoon. And then, after serving Liturgy on Sunday morning, I would return.

The Elder had the amazing zeal to imitate the different ascetic practices of the saints he had read about in the *synaxaria*. He read the life of St. Daniel the Stylite, who kept his continence for many days because of the many pilgrims that besieged him day and night for his counsel or his blessing. Amazed by the superhuman asceticism of the Saint, he became "envious" of him with a righteous zeal.

> From the time I left the monastery to go and liturgize in the different villages, I kept my continence until I returned to the monastery. I stayed at the houses of different pious people on Saturday evenings, but in many of the villages there was not a dedicated

> place to use the restroom—the villagers would use the fields outside of the village to relieve themselves. Even if there were dedicated restrooms, one had to be very careful because for priests everything is an opportunity to be misunderstood. So, imitating the "violence"[16] of the saints, I was extremely strict with myself on this matter.

The following account makes it apparent how watchful the Elder was to maintain the purity of his heart. For however many children he baptized in the surrounding area, throughout the sacrament he never looked at their naked bodies.

> I baptized all of them with my eyes closed. And when I chrismated them or cut their hair during the tonsure, I did it with my eyes closed. I was careful to never let my soul be imprinted at all with the naked body, even that of an infant child.

Many times, according to the blessed custom of those days, the Elder would take the holy skull of St. David to bless the surrounding area. Fr. Iakovos would process from village to village on donkeys from the monastery, which was a very tiring and difficult task for the hesychast. But when the Elder finished these tours and returned to the monastery, many times he would see St. David and would receive a reward from the Saint for his labor. The Elder said:

> One time, returning with the holy skull, I spent the night outside of the monastery. As I approached, I saw a bright light outside of the monastery that was illuminating the area and the path I was taking. As soon as I arrived, I went into the church and saw, off to the right, an older monk waiting for me. After

---

16 Matthew 11:12.

I returned the saint's skull and venerated the icons on the icon screen, I looked for this older monk to greet him, thinking that it was one of the fathers of the monastery. But he disappeared. It was St. David waiting for me, alive as he is.

On his liturgical excursions the Elder couldn't believe the great poverty and needs of the churches and chapels of the area. With zeal and sacrifices, he used every coin that God gave him to furnish the churches with everything they needed, including liturgical vessels. He succeeded in this task, as he confessed joyfully, by seeing all the churches put in good order, equipped, furnished, and with every need fulfilled. He even provided for the vigil lamps in the churches by sharing the oil of the monastery.

The Elder shares a miracle related to this:

> We did not have much oil for the monastery; there were many churches in the area, and there were many poor people that we gave oil to because they could not afford any. I begged Panagia, St. David, and Prophet Elias to help us have enough oil to share with everyone.
>
> After praying, I went down to the area where oil was stored in the monastery. I saw the oil jar shaking, and oil was spilling out of the top and down the side. At first, I thought a mouse had gotten into the jar, had tried to get out, and in the process had knocked off the lid and spilled the oil. I thought to myself, "Now what am I going to do?"
>
> If a mouse got into the oil we couldn't use it for cooking or even for the vigil lamps. I was confused: I couldn't understand how the mouse fell in because the lid clearly was in place.

I lifted the lid and, to my disbelief, not only was there no mouse inside the jar; but the oil was miraculously bubbling and overflowing out of the jar, like water flows out of a spring and floods the area around it. This miracle happened specifically because we were trying to provide enough oil for the surrounding churches and chapels and to give as charity to the poor.

The practice of charity and almsgiving was an inheritance that the Elder received from his mother. This virtue, which made God man,[17] so enriched the soul of the Elder that there were several miraculous events that took place. He especially encouraged his spiritual children to open their hearts and their hands to give with joy and then to see the miracles that would occur in their lives. The Elder "bartered" with the Merciful God; he emptied his hands and God filled them again even more. The Elder would share it all and then the Merciful One would respond with even greater gifts. The Elder was marveled and stunned by the immensity of this virtue and the richness of the Mercy of God.[18]

One time the Elder was serving Liturgy in one of the villages nearby. He concluded and began his return trip to the monastery on one of the donkeys, with around ten to twenty drachmas in his pocket. On the road he saw an old woman sitting outside of a house, under a tree soaking wet and shivering, covered only by a sack. Because he had just undergone surgery, he got down with difficulty from the

---

17 The ultimate act of charity, the ultimate gift of mercy, is the Incarnation. "In this the love of God was manifested toward us, that God has sent His only begotten Son into the world, that we might live through Him." 1 Jn. 4:9. (TN)

18 In Greek, the connection that St. Iakovos is drawing is more easily recognized: almsgiving (ἡ ἐλεημοσύνη) is derived from the word for mercy (τό ἔλεος). (TN)

donkey to comfort her, because he thought this was his duty. He recognized the woman because he knew her son and his wife. He told her:

> "Take these twenty drachmas and go buy some sugar, boil some water, and make a warm drink. I don't have anything else to give you but hopefully this money will help."

After comforting her, he mounted his donkey and continued towards the monastery. A little further along the road he encountered another older woman he knew who stopped him and said:

> "Fr. Iakovos, please take this money and these eggs as tokens of my gratitude for remembering my departed husband when you commemorate names during the *proskomide*."

And she handed him 200 drachmas and quite a lot of eggs.

The Elder told her, "Sweet lady, I would pray for your husband regardless; I don't want money. As for the eggs, we have chickens at the monastery; please keep them." The woman replied, "Please Father, don't insult me by refusing these gifts." So the Elder was obliged to keep them.

He arrived at the monastery and immediately he saw a sick, old man from one of the neighboring villages waiting. He implored, "Fr. Iakovos: if you have it, could you loan me 100 drachmas so I can go to the doctor? I will repay you whenever I can."

Then the Elder told him, "Take these 200 drachmas for the doctor and for medicine, but I don't want you to repay me."

As Fr. Iakovos entered the monastery, with his pockets now empty again, some visitors approached him and said,

"Elder, take this envelope and pray for us during forty liturgies." And they handed him 2,000 drachmas.

"I will do forty liturgies, but I don't want the money." However they begged him to keep it. The Elder then used the money to buy a candlestand for the monastery and whatever was left over he distributed to the poor.

> Every month I would distribute alms to families to help provide for their basic needs, either in the form of food or in money. I would give one and then God would give me ten. As soon as I thought of giving something immediately God would answer me and would multiply it.

The Elder toiled with superhuman efforts to sustain his service of charity with care for people's material and spiritual needs. His entire wondrous life, with his spiritual and bodily struggles, was based on his Orthodox faith. Particular events and practices of the wise and discerning Elder confirm the precise observance of the dogmatic teaching of the Church. The Elder taught in practice. Let's refer to one of the many such examples.

When an adherent of Catholicism expressed a desire to become Orthodox, he told him, "what prevents you to be baptized?"[19] Out of respect to the ecclesiastical hierarchy he counseled us to go to the bishop of the area and to announce the man's decision. "You will go to the bishop who, immediately upon hearing of your decision, will rise from his throne and embrace you, my child, out of joy that you want to become Orthodox." In saying this, he was actually describing his own spiritual state and desire. To our great surprise, we were not able to even see the face of the bishop! Through his deacon, he communicated to us that, according to a decision of the Holy Synod [of the Church

---

19 Acts 8:36

of Greece], the baptism of Latins is valid and does not need to be repeated. He simply needs to sign a written confession and the Mystery of Chrismation is to be performed.

When we informed the Elder of this, he said: "I don't know what the Holy Synod decided. I know what the Gospel says: 'He that believeth and is baptized shall be saved.'"[20] He said this and went and brought a large baptismal font, appropriate for adults, from nearby Limni, Evia. In the chapel of St. Haralambos, which was the cell of Saint David of Evia, the Holy Elder performed the Mystery of Baptism with great splendour, and also the Mystery of Chrismation according to the Orthodox Typikon, with help of the Archimandrite Father Paul Ioannou, his spiritual child, who later became the Metropolitan of Siatista. I, the author, was the godfather (sponsor).

The Elder's health up until he was 55 years old was strong as iron despite his sick constitution.[21] Eventually the time arrived when God allowed the Elder to suffer many and painful illnesses because, as the Elder explained, "Lucifer received permission to torment my body."[22] He knew this because a demon that had possessed a woman revealed this to the Elder. The demon told him that the demon's "father," that is Lucifer, had received permission to torment the Elder's body and proceeded to list specific difficulties that only the Elder knew.

> Since I was a small child, I had been seen naked only by my mother. But God allowed doctors and nurses to see me unclothed due to my frequent surgeries. I began to feel pain in different parts of my body. I didn't want to go to the doctor at first because I

---

20 Mark 16:16

21 In this section, the author, who was St. Iakovos' physician, records the specific nature of the saint's physical ailments with medical detail. (TN)

22 Job 2:5-6.

thought it was shameful for them to see my body, the body of a priest.

Fr. Iakovos' Elder, Fr. Nikodemos, told him, "My child, go to the doctor. God has allowed you to fall into this serious suffering because you are prideful and you won't undergo an examination."

"My Elder, what pride? I am embarrassed to be seen naked."

One time they grabbed me and forced me up on the top of a donkey. They took me down to Limni and then to a hospital in Chalkida. There a surgeon examined me and pronounced, "Emergency surgery." I was truly in a bad situation and I prayed to St. David, saying:

> My Saint David, I beg you to quickly come here in ten minutes to help me. Come by way of Prokopi, bring St. John the Russian[23] with you, and please come and help me because I am in great danger.

I prayed for this in my heart. Not a few minutes passed when the door opened and an old, white-bearded man holding a cane entered together with a younger looking man around 30 years old in a black robe. They came to me and greeted me. I thought they were some priests from the town because many

---

23 St. John the Russian, like St. Iakovos and St. David, was another saint that showed a yearning for holiness from a young age. Enslaved by a Turkish Aga, he was encouraged to apostatize, but he resisted and maintained an active prayer life as a Christian in the service of a Muslim family. He worked many miracles in his life and reposed in peace on 27 May 1730. His relics were a treasure to the residents of Prokopi in Asia Minor. During their flight to mainland Greece these were brought by the villagers and now reside in New Prokopi on the island of Evia. (TN)

priests had come to visit me in the hospital after they heard I was very sick.

> The older monk said to me, "How are you, Fr. Iakovos? Do you know who we are?"
>
> "What am I to do? I'm bearing it as well as I can," I told them. "I don't know who you are."
>
> "I am St. David and here is John the Confessor. Right, John?" he said, directing his word towards the younger priest. St. John nodded and bowed slightly to St. David, acknowledging him out of deference to his age and his priesthood.
>
> "Don't be afraid," St. David said. "We came to help you."

I could see that St. David's forehead was sweating; that was how quickly the Saint came to help me. I turned to my abbot and elder Fr. Nikodemos, who was next to me, and said,

> "My Elder, here are St. David and St. John the Russian."
>
> Then my elder leaned his ear next to me and said to me, "What are you saying? Have you gone crazy? What St. David are you talking about? Don't say things like that. If anyone hears you, they'll say that Fr. Iakovos has lost his mind."

When I realized that my elder didn't see anything, I was quiet. I saw St. David go ahead and enter the surgery suite. He used his staff to open the door and I saw him and St. John standing next to me at the surgery table.

> With the anesthesia I fell asleep and didn't understand what was going on. The surgeon was truly in a difficult situation. He had to perform three surgeries simultaneously because my appendix burst, I had a testicular torsion, and I had suffered an inguinal hernia. With the help of the saints and the earnest efforts of the good surgeon, I was saved. As I woke up, I said repeatedly, "A very good surgeon saved me."
>
> Then I heard and saw St. John the Russian say to me, "You're only talking about the surgeon, but you should thank me because I was the one who did the surgery. Yesterday you were going to die but you got an extension till tomorrow."
>
> So, with this "extension" I am still alive.

Later the Elder had severe varicose veins on his legs and feet that required surgery in Athens. Again, the situation was extremely dire. The Elder suffered so badly from his legs that the endurance and spiritual vigor it required just to stand up was unbelievable—even looking at them was pitiable. But he never missed any of the divine services, defying all the instructions of his doctors to avoid standing up. In the evenings, after a full day of labor, the pain was unimaginable, and no human help could be of use.

> My good Panagia would come with St. David and put medicine on my legs and the pain would go away after a few hours. In the morning, however, the pain would start again.

One of the greatest trials of the Elder was the sporadic rashes he would experience in his private areas, even into the end of his intestinal tube. It would become very irritated at times which led to excruciating pain and an unbearable itch.

> That little itch was truly an attack from the devil. The pain I could bear, my child, but the itch was almost unbearable. It was especially bad when I would be vested and ready to serve one of the services. It was so unbearable I would become drenched in a cold sweat. If it was possible, I would have used a razor and scraped off my skin—I would have preferred to be in pain than to have this itch. But what was I to do? I bore this trial with patience.

The Elder was also tormented with vertigo in his last years, which was caused by the neck injury he had sustained as a younger man.

> I didn't dare turn my head to the side in the event that everything would start spinning; I had to keep it totally still, in one place. This was especially difficult during the seemingly endless hours of hearing confessions when I would have sharp pain in my neck. This was an ascetic struggle—I wouldn't turn my head up to see the face of the person confessing; I would keep my head bowed in the same position patiently.

This trial of illnesses did not even leave his digestive system intact—he suffered from a perforated intestine that led to extreme abdominal pain and bloating. Even his urinary system was not left unaffected. One time when he was catheterized the nurse was not careful when she performed the procedure (or perhaps it was the devil who mischievously intervened). The nurse inserted the wrong catheter size, which not only caused great pain but also scarred the Elder's urethra and impacted his ability to urinate. Because of this injury, whatever little rest the Elder had at night was interrupted every hour or so because his bladder could not empty normally.

The last struggle that finally led the Elder to the next life was his heart issues.

> My heart did not have any problems. It was a temptation of the devil that I felt attack me one time while speaking with a priest. It was a pain like a knife in the chest and I realized at that moment that my heart was very sick. Eventually I had to have a pacemaker put in. It took two surgeries for it to be implanted. The first one was not successful and the second one I did without anesthesia. Eventually the pacemaker was implanted, but too close to my right armpit which gave me pain every time I made my Cross or picked up the Gospel.

The Elder's myocardial ischemia was very serious and despite the medicine, appointments, and emergency visits to the hospital in Athens, the situation continued to get worse. The heat and the cold caused him great pain in his chest, which would be followed by sweats and exhaustion. But the Elder's zeal and his love for God and His creation kept his much-afflicted body upright until his final hour. He was patient, with a smile on his lips and with the love to serve others ceaselessly. He softened hard hearts; he enlightened, warmed, and healed souls and bodies, pouring out wine and oil[24] as a true disciple of the Physician of our souls and bodies.

The ascetic Fr. Iakovos, who was humble, meek, and quiet, became a teacher using soft and mellifluous words in his last years through the enlightenment of the Holy Spirit. Whoever met him perceived a certain joy within themselves when listening to him speak. Sometimes he

---

24 Luke 10:25-37.

would speak about his life, childhood, and family life. Other times he would speak with fervor about his much beloved St. David. And at other times, he would give spiritual counsel about specific problems the faithful would bring before him—problems he knew about in advance without having to be told by the one suffering. This gift of insight is one that countless events bear witness to, through his personal communication with his spiritual children. Pilgrims were astounded when, after first meeting the Elder, he would call them by their nicknames and begin speaking to them about their specific problems before miraculously presenting them with solutions and directions. In other instances, he would reveal their hidden passions and sins but in a joking way so as not to embarrass them. In his explanation he was always full of joy. He spoke with childlike simplicity and the joy that spread around him was so immense, so full of the Resurrection, that people sitting or standing around him begged him to keep speaking when he would stop. They felt such a blessing to be close to him, to see him, and to hear him.

After finishing the Divine Liturgy, the Elder would go to the dining hall where the faithful could eat together or drink a cup or two of coffee. It would take him an hour and a half to walk those 65 feet because of all the people, of every age, that would stop him. Even after a very long Divine Liturgy, he would smile at everyone and try to give them at least one word of comfort. He would wait patiently, standing upright, in the courtyard of the monastery until he could make it to his little chair in the dining hall. One cannot imagine how much pain was hidden by the Elder's smile. Many visitors to the monastery did not know how poor his health was, and they congratulated him on looking so good. All his good efforts happened in secret. Underneath his kind words, his paternal love, and the heavenly sweetness of his face, there was an ascetic who was being willingly crucified, just as it says in the hymn: "Holy Father, you did not allow yourself to remain a clay vessel, but you were transformed by tribulations and became like brass and were put to good use by the Master Christ."

The Elder, who up until then had remained unknown to the world, was flooded in his last years by visitors and pilgrims from Greece and abroad. A multitude of people of every social class flocked to him: from the uneducated to university professors; from judges and politicians to shepherds, carpenters, monks, and clergy of every level. In the face of the Elder they saw a man of God who gave them relief, who put them at ease, who inspired them, and who gave them hope and joy. With only a word he could bring them peace.

The Elder's miraculous life was worthy of a holy repose. Like his mother, he was aware of his death before it happened. In the morning a deacon from Mount Athos had visited him for confession, and the Elder asked him to stay until the afternoon to help him get dressed. The last day of his earthly life was especially joyful. On the morning of November 21, the feast of the Entrance of the Theotokos, he did not serve Divine Liturgy; but he chanted and received the Holy Mysteries. Around four in the afternoon, which was the time he normally heard confessions, with his *epitrachelion* on his neck—that *epitrachelion* that had refreshed and renewed us spiritually so many times, which had sweetened us, which had relieved us of such great weight—he flew like a pure dove accompanied by the saints of his heart: St. David, St. John the Russian, St. Haralambos, and Lord knows how many other ascetics and righteous monastics of similar disposition. He was brought before the slain lamb, to his sweetest Jesus, his one and only true love so that he could intercede for all of us ceaselessly. He left this world for eternal rest without having rested his body. He left at the time of the mystery of confession and mercy. He didn't have time to read that last prayer of forgiveness so that he would be worthy of interceding for us face-to-face for all our sins. All of us that were at his funeral service truly felt that "the grace of the Holy Spirit has brought us together."[25] We did not experience the grief of worldly separation as much as we truly experienced the joy of the Resurrection. We are sure that we have an Advocate before the Lord: our Holy Elder, our Father Iakovos, to intercede day and night for all of us.

O Father Iakovos, you who showed us through your life the gifts of the Holy Spirit, you who loved us, do not cease interceding for the fathers of your Holy Monastery, for us your spiritual children, and for the soul of every Christian who is fighting the good fight in Christ. Amen.

---

25   First *Idiomelon* at the Vespers of Palm Sunday. (TN)

This miraculous image was taken of the cell of Saint Iakovos 11 months after his repose. Upon developing the film, the photographer was amazed to see the Saint appearing as if present.

CHAPTER 5
Stories and Visions of Father Iakovos

ICONS ARE VESSELS OF GRACE

The grace of our saints is even in the wood of the holy icons. Back in our homeland of Asia Minor there was a Turkish shepherd who, every time he would milk his sheep, would cover the milk pail with a large and heavily chipped piece of wood from an icon of Panagia. The colors had disappeared over the years and it had become so disfigured it looked like a plain piece of wood. The following miracle happened: one morning when the Turk went to his sheepfold, he found the milk bucket turned over, the milk spilled out, and the icon standing up against a tree. At first, he could not explain what had happened, because the milk was still flowing. He said angrily, "Maybe that wood is spilling it," because he knew it had been an old icon from the Christians.

He grabbed his axe to cut the icon so that he could burn it. With the first strike of the axe the icon began to bleed. The blood began to flow out of the cut. The Turk, terrified and shaking, tried to remove the axe but he could not pull it out because it was so deep. He threw the ax with the icon on his shoulder and ran until he got to the village. Some Christians who saw the miracle took the icon, which had brought the Turk to fearful tears, and they properly honored it.

Panagia Xenia Returns

Later in my life, when I was suffering from vertigo, I was informed that the icon of Panagia Xenia of Almyros was visiting Limni in Evia. Even though I was sick, I felt obligated to Panagia because she had healed my feet as a child, so I went to venerate the icon out of gratitude. There was a procession with the miracle-working icon, and the other priests let me go first because I was a priest-monk. I did not want to go first or have any special honors, but I did not have a choice and was obedient to their request. During the procession, we stopped to say the petitions and it was my turn to say the final exclamation, "Hear us O God, our Savior, the hope of all the ends of the earth." Then I saw in the icon our Panagia was alive. She turned her head with her large eyes and looked at me, raised her hand and blessed me. I lost my voice and my feet stopped; with great difficulty I continued, "Hear us our God, hear us our God," repeatedly. God only knows how I finished the petition and continued in the procession. Panagia was alive, in her holy icon; I saw her with my eyes!

St. Nicholas Galataki

The Elder recalled a story from the Monastery of St. Nicholas Galataki[26] from when it was still a men's monastery. There was an impious shepherd that would tend his sheep together with the monastery's sheep and then give the

---

26 This monastery is found a few kilometers outside of Limni and is the oldest monastery on the island, probably founded as early as the eighth century. It was a men's monastery until 1946 and eventually became a women's monastery. (TN)

monastery their portion of the cheese and wool generated by the flock. One time in a truly evil way, this man unjustly took the portion of the herd that was for the monastery and kept it for himself—refusing to give them their fair share. He would not repent of this despite the begging and requests of the monks who were destitute and greatly depended on the income. One Sunday after the Liturgy, the abbot of the monastery, fully vested, took a censer and an icon of St. Nicholas and went up to a hill overlooking the village of the unrighteous shepherd. It was a beautiful day, perfect for threshing, and all the villagers were threshing wheat from their fields. The abbot lifted his hands in prayer, with the icon of St. Nicholas facing the village, and he prayed:

> *O my Saint Nicholas, if you are a miracle-worker, which we know you to be, then bring punishment on this man who has defrauded your monastery because we truly needed what he stole from us!*

The sky was completely clear, and the sun was shining, but then a loud thunderclap was heard, and a bolt of lightning struck the evil shepherd's threshing floor and burned him, his family, and all of his livestock without harming any of the other villagers nearby who were threshing. Truly, "It is a terrifying thing to fall into the hands of the living God."[27]

STOLEN OLIVES

One time someone came and cut down some olive trees that belonged to the monastery. I was upset and went to St. David. I said to him:

> My Saint, I came here to your monastery to serve you; I can't be preoccupied with the monastery's olive trees. You go and find the person who did this

---

27 Hebrews 10:31.

and bring them to me by this afternoon. If you don't help me with this, I won't cense you!

Immediately the bones of the saint moved and his icon turned black. That icon is alive and many times it would change expression and color according to the disposition of the saint. That afternoon, out of nowhere, a terrified old man came to the monastery shaking and asking to see me. I went and met with him alone, and he revealed to me that he had cut the olive trees of the monastery and he had come to repent. The saint brought him just as I had asked.

The Instruments of the Devil

God has his own people, but the devil also uses people as instruments of evil. One of the local shepherds was a source of great temptation for the meek Elder. Some of the shepherd's sheep were attacked and eaten by wild dogs, but he believed that it was a dog from the monastery that was tied up and guarded the monastery chickens. Even though the Elder confirmed that it was impossible, the shepherd still blamed this dog. He filed a formal complaint in court: "The Archimandrite, Fr. Iakovos Tsalikis, who has packs of dogs, was the cause of the slaughter of my herd." The Elder was very worried.

He was in the courtyard of the monastery when he saw a very thin, sickly bird perched on the wall looking down at him. Immediately it flew to the roof of the monastery and said,

> "I brought you that call to court. It was I who caused it all."

It was the devil in the form of a bird. The Elder was worried about going to the courtroom because it would have been shameful for a priest. In the end, with the support of a lawyer and the help of St. David, he did not have to go to trial and the situation was put in order.

The Devil at Work

Another time I was at the entrance of the monastery and I saw an old woman come in. I greeted her, saying:

> "Come, dear granny, so we can treat you and give you something to eat, give you food to take home and help you with whatever you need. Come venerate the relics in the church first and stay the evening; we can give you a small room to yourself to rest in."

Then, this person who appeared like an old woman, responded:

> "Ba! I'm not staying here. I can't stay here because you're always *boom, boom,* ringing the bells. I only came here to see you and then I'm leaving. I am going to this women's monastery," and she told me which one. "There they give me a great welcome and I will stay for a week."

I thought to myself, as a woman, this granny would feel more relaxed at a women's monastery; that's why she does not want to stay here. We were talking like this as we were walking to the entrance of the church. The old woman continued:

> "As soon as I get to the monastery, I will start doing this to the nuns," and then she gestured with her finger like she was going to skewer them. "And then the scandals and problems will start between them and that's when the party really starts."

I was taken aback by what she was saying, so I took a closer look at her face. I noticed that she had very small, beady eyes covered in makeup. She was wearing giant earrings and her nose was pierced by a chain that connected to the earrings. I made my Cross immediately, saying, "Lord have mercy, what old woman is this?!" Immediately she began to melt and disappeared before me like smoke.

I went and told the other monks, "I just saw the devil and spoke to him, thinking it was an old woman," and then explained what he had said to me.

The Elder noted that having daily services, especially serving the Divine Liturgy daily, kept the devil far away. The devil testified that he could not stay at the Elder's monastery because of the continuous ringing of the bells and how much he rejoiced in the scandals and misunderstandings elsewhere that for him were a big party. The Elder would say that the devil always came to the monastery but could never find someone unprotected so he could not stay and do his evil work.

One time we were praying the Small Compline with the fathers in my cell. I opened the door to go outside and I saw the devil appearing again as an immodest woman. She turned around and showed her "backside" saying shameless words. I grabbed my icon of Panagia and went outside, saying, *Under your compassion we take refuge, O Theotokos...*[28] And then, like a bullet whistling out of a gun, the devil was shot over the roof of the monastery and exploded on the hill across the valley with a loud, echoing noise.

Another morning, as the sun was beginning to rise, I came out of my cell to head to the church. I saw a huge black dog standing outside of my door. Before I left the door of my cell, I made the sign of the Cross like I always do. I shook the dog a little with my foot and said, "You're sleeping

---

[28] The final *troparion* chanted during the Compunctionate Vespers of Great Lent. (TN)

here, outside?" While I walked I said the Jesus Prayer, "Lord Jesus Christ Son of God have mercy on me," and was making my Cross over and over again. I turned around and the dog had disappeared. It was the devil who was waiting for me, hoping to throw me down the stairs. But the power of the Precious Cross protected me.

PROPER ATTIRE

It is important when people come to visit monasteries and churches to be dressed modestly and properly. One time a young scientist, a rural doctor, came to visit the monastery wearing a short-sleeved shirt. At that moment there was a demon-possessed woman sitting in the courtyard of the monastery. She came and grabbed him by the arm and held him with incredible strength saying, "Hey, you atheist. You don't believe in anything. Are you going to write me a recipe for curing people, you who came to me wearing that t-shirt?" The Elder described how hard it was to get him out of the hands of this demon-possessed woman, and how the poor man left completely terrified.

GOOD ROOTS

The Elder often described the importance of the spiritual state and the life of parents, grandparents, and other ancestors to the spiritual development of future generations. The Elder descended from a family tree that was a blessed inheritor from the passage of time—holy people, dedicated to God. He also spoke from the experience of having spent many years interacting with families, witnessing how bad situations and the passions could hurt even children and grandchildren. The Elder counseled parents to pray as much as possible for their children and to encourage their children to interact with virtuous families. "Roots are of great importance," he would often say.

The Elder demonstrates the importance of this generational holiness when he describes the saint that his family had produced.

> Two siblings from our extended family decided to leave for the Holy Lands and dedicate themselves to God. One of them stayed for a little bit and then took his bag and left. The other went in to venerate the Holy Sepulcher and didn't leave the Church of the Resurrection. He stayed the rest of his life there as a monastic in the brotherhood of the Holy Sepulcher as a reclusive ascetic. The Patriarch of Jerusalem, seeing his holy life, permitted him to live there and in this way he pleased God.

CHANGING AN OBEDIENCE

A spiritual father is not allowed to change the canon of obedience given by another spiritual father. One time an old woman came to me for confession, and I gave her the rule that she could not receive Holy Communion for three years. The priest and the spiritual father at the parish where the woman attended church asked her why she was not communing and she explained to them it was because Fr. Iakovos had put her under a rule.

"Why did he give you that rule?" he asked her.

When she told him the reason, the priest replied,

> "No, no, dear granny, don't worry. Fr. Iakovos is an uneducated monk. I am a well-studied and educated priest and I remove this rule from you. Come on Sunday and receive Holy Communion."

When the granny went on Sunday and received Holy Communion, she felt in her mouth that—as she described it—"a cold and empty spoon," with no taste, entered her mouth. This really caught her attention. When the same thing happened two more Sundays, she was concerned and returned to the monastery, confessing all these things to me. She said that, because the other priest had dissolved the rule, she had communed three times but without actually communing: the spoon was empty and cold. I told her, "My child, a rule of obedience like that cannot be dissolved. You must fulfill the rule that I gave you. The canons must be applied."

The Sacred Altar

There were countless miracles the Elder experienced during his many years of hearing confessions. Let us report some of them.

One time an old woman came to me and told me that she went to light the vigil lamps in one of the chapels on Holy and Great Friday. Out of an idle curiosity, she put her head through the little door and looked into the Holy Altar. Sitting on top of the Holy Table, she saw a young man around 30 years old that had deep wounds on his palms, his feet, and one more on his side. Blood was flowing out of all of them.

Stunned, the granny started asking him, "Who are you and how dare you sit on top of the Holy Table?"

He replied, "I am always sitting here, because this is my place."

Then the granny said to him, "Who wounded you so?"

He replied, "You wounded me like this—with your sins."

This woman was made worthy to see the Lord, and she was repentant the rest of her life.

Another older woman went, apparently without any respect, into the Holy Altar to clean it. To quickly clean all the spider webs from the ceiling, she dared to stand on top of the Holy Altar table. As soon as she put her foot on top of the table, she felt burning, sharp needles on her feet. Immediately, she fell, broke her leg, and within a few days, she died.

Holy Communion

One time a well-known person came to stay at the monastery and, while we were talking, he told me that he was planning to receive Holy Communion during Divine Liturgy the following day. I could see that he should not commune because he had not confessed in a long time and his sins prevented him from receiving Holy Communion. During our conversation, I tried to give him the opportunity to confess, but it was impossible. All night I could not sleep, thinking about how I could not commune him: wouldn't it be quite offensive to deny him Holy Communion? When it came time for the man to approach, unworthily, I saw a gold beam of light flash and fly out of the spoon, over the shoulder of the priest, and onto the Holy Table. The flash of light was the holy particle that left. The man didn't actually commune, which naturally would have been to his condemnation.

Whenever I commune people, I never look them in the face. However, a few times I would have the thought to look at their faces as they received Holy Communion. Sometimes I would see a person approaching not with the face of a man but with the face of a dog, other times like a monkey, or faces of other animals, terrifying faces. "My God," I would think to myself, "how do they have the faces of animals?" There were other times I would see people come forward to commune with peaceful and joyful faces, and after they communed their faces would shine like the sun.

I saw the face of a priest in the holy altar completely black, and another time I saw a bishop serving the Divine Liturgy and he was black all over like tar. I saw another young person studying to become a priest, and I understood from looking at him that he did not have even the right to stand in the church or move around the church, let alone receive the Pure Mysteries.

One time I saw on the paten a clot of blood, and I showed it to one of the other monks and in a little while it disappeared. People are blind and do not see what is happening in the church during the Divine Liturgy. Another time I was serving and I could not do the Great Entrance because of what I saw. The chanter kept saying over and over again, "That we may receive the King of all." Suddenly, I felt someone push me by the shoulder and guide me to the table of oblation. I thought it was the chanter and assumed that he had irreverently gone in through the Beautiful Gates and pushed me. I turned around and saw a giant wing of the Archangel that had pushed on my shoulder and guided me to do the Great Entrance. The things that happen inside of the holy altar during the Divine Liturgy... Sometimes I could not bear what I saw and would sit down in a chair; those who were serving with me thought something was wrong with my health, but they did not see or hear what I did. O how the angels flutter their wings, my child! As soon as the priest says, "Through the prayers of the holy fathers..." the heavenly powers leave and in the holy altar is complete silence.

The Elder's Words

One time the Elder said to one of his spiritual children, "Today when you communed, did you see how you felt? It is always like this for me. Christ is always inside of me."

The Elder told his spiritual child, "Do not be prideful, my child. When you communed today your face shone like the sun. With these good transformations a person is protected from pride."

The Elder also said, "My body is dead—better that way, instead of suffering evil now that I am aged."

The Elder spoke about an incident while he was in the hospital, "One time when I was in the hospital, one of my spiritual children—who was a priest—served a vigil for my health. When this priest left the church and started to head for the hospital to commune me, although I was in the hospital, I could feel inside my soul that my Christ was coming, that Holy Communion was coming."

One time, one of the Elder's spiritual children was with him when one of the buttons on his shirt accidently came undone and opened a little immodestly. The Elder said to him, "Button your shirt, my child, so that you do not get cold." That is how much the Elder kept and guarded modesty.

Obedience always burns the devil. One time, the same spiritual child happened to meet someone who was probably possessed by a demon. This person said, "Hey, come on. Undo that button because you look like an idiot." And then the spiritual child remembered the counsel of his Elder, even during this seemingly unimportant event.

Another time the Elder told someone, "I am so happy, my child, to see you with long sleeves, modest and attentive to your appearance."

The Elder told one of his spiritual children, "The devil came to me and told me what sins you committed."

To one of his spiritual children who was mentally "going" to church very frequently, the Elder said, "I am not seeing things, but I see your soul is always inside of the church, inside my cell, and so on."

Priests and Priests' Wives

The Elder said, "If I see a priest with cut hair, a trimmed beard, and wearing cologne, I don't even want to greet him. Priests should not cut their hair." The Elder explained, "Back in Asia Minor, when the priests combed their hair or their beard, they would put a white towel down and whatever hairs fell there they collected and put in a small bag. When the priest died, they would put that bag with him because, when the Holy Spirit descended on him, the priest became holy and even the hairs on his head were holy." One of the Elder's spiritual children heard this and thought to himself, "Okay, fine, they gathered their hairs. But what about when they trimmed their fingernails—what did they do? Did they throw them away?" Then the Elder turned his head and said to him, "And yes, they did gather their fingernails." Nothing is hidden to the Holy Spirit; everything appears to Him clearly and readily.

The wives of priests must live a holy life, almost like a monastic, with a great respect for the priest and with modest appearance. The Elder explained that, in Asia Minor, the priest's wife always dressed in her most simple and plain clothes while baking *prosforo* with her head covered; basically like a nun. When she would go to church, she would go to the north gate, make a prostration to her husband the priest, kiss his hand, and give him the *prosforo*. Then she would go to her place. Because of her modest conduct she was a very well-respected person and had a high reputation with the people. The Elder particularly advised the wives of priests to not avoid personal attacks from people, because in doing so these temptations may attack the priest who is the main target of the devil.[29]

The Elder said, "No one should be ordained who has some impediment to the priesthood. One time, I saw a priest whose ordination I had earlier supported. But I later learned that he had not made a full confession before coming a priest. After four years he told me about this sin, which was an impediment. His face was so sad and black; he had no joy. His situation really bothered me."

Regarding unmarried priests that live in the world, serving in churches, the Elder said, "If someone has the holiness of St. David, he can help people through confession, and so on. But like the saint, he must return to his ascetic life; otherwise, it is impossible for celibate clergy to live in the world. Maybe only one in a thousand unmarried priests is really pleasing to God."

The Elder would advise people coming for confession that they should not share with anyone the content of their confession, or their spiritual labor, because then God will depart. He will become a laughingstock to everyone when people see that his life is much different than his words. Everything should happen in secret and according to the advice of only the spiritual father.

Someone came to the Elder once and said, "I do three thousand prostrations every day." "Good job, my child," the Elder replied. "But from now on you will only do 100 prostrations, because if you keep that up later on in life you will be too tired to do any."

---

29 There is a spiritual "law," supported by countless people, that the devil attacks married priests through their wives and children meaning to ultimately destroy the priest so he cannot aid souls along the path of salvation. These attacks distract the priest from his calling by weighing him down by the concerns of family life. The burden born by the clergy family is a great one that should not be undertaken lightly, and the lay people have a special responsibility to uphold the families of their priests in prayer. (TN)

The Elder said, "In our prayers, we should be very careful about what exactly we are asking for; because we do not know if he will give us what we are asking for and if we will be able to endure it. Someone prayed to be absolved from a sin by getting cancer, and then He actually got cancer. We must be very careful what we ask for in our prayers."

Someone who was serving with the Elder told him that he felt like he was burned when he communed. The Elder replied, "When I commune, I do not feel like it burns me. When I am preparing the gifts before Divine Liturgy, I see souls pass before me and beg me to commemorate them; and even if I wanted to forget them, I couldn't."

Children

The Elder would counsel parents not to let their children hang out with other groups of children and go about town. Rather he thought it better for children to stay with their parents, even if it meant they would be characterized by others as "antisocial." He counseled children to never take anything from strangers: not candy or soda or anything else, because of the great number of kids getting hooked on drugs which was decimating the youth of that time. Also, because of the danger of AIDS at that time, before the mode of transmission of HIV was fully understood, he counseled people to be careful shaking hands with strangers and encouraged us to wash our hands very well and even use a little alcohol because God gave us a brain. He counseled us that, when we were sick, to go to the doctor and be obedient to the course of therapy. He shared that one Lent, during the whole Fast, he counted that he had taken about 600 pills. We should be careful with our health because God gave us doctors and medicines and we should not ignore them.[30]

---

30 The saint's experience with his physicians, including the author of this present biography, should judiciously be extended to 21st century public

Televisions

About television, he was uncompromising.

"Television is very damaging, especially to children, and it should be removed from the house," he said.

One time one of his spiritual children, a small child, begged him during confession to be allowed to watch a few educational and children's shows. But the Elder would not give him a blessing; he was unwavering:

> "No television in the house. For the news you can have a radio, which your parents can listen to."

On Dresses or Pants for Girls

The Elder advised that little girls should not wear pants but should wear dresses or skirts. He only gave an exception for exercise or sports.

Eternal Life

When my Elder, Fr. Nikodemos, reposed, I asked in my prayer, "Where is his soul going to go?" Then I saw, not in a dream but in a spiritual manner, that my elder was yelling for me to bring the keys to the monastery because the Great High Priest was coming. I went to his cell, which was above the entrance to the monastery, and standing outside the door

---

health challenges. The Saint trusted the advice of his doctors while putting his total faith in God and His Saints as evidenced by the many miraculous healings that the Saint experienced. The only way to truly know how St. Iakovos or other holy people would respond to our modern problems is to approach them patiently and humbly in prayer to ask for their guidance. The saints, as St. Iakovos demonstrates, are not distant historical figures but our close friends and advocates on the journey to salvation. We do not need to imagine how St. Iakovos would deal with a particular problem, we can incline the knee of our heart and implore him for guidance in our own lives. (TN)

I could hear speeches, questions, and responses. Inside an examination was occurring, an interrogation. I knocked on the door, and what did I see! My elder was standing upright, with his head uncovered, his head bowed down, and his hands crossed with fear and reverence. Across from him was the Great High Priest sitting on a throne. The throne was floating above the floor and His face was shining gold, like a clean candle; I couldn't possibly describe it. At his knees was an open book and inside was written my elder's entire life. The Great High Priest would ask a question and then my elder would reply. As soon as I went inside, the interrogation stopped. I went to my elder, made a prostration to him, and then gave him the keys to the monastery.

"Elder, I brought the keys for the holy relics in case the High Priest wants to venerate them." My Elder took the keys. I wanted to make a prostration to the Great High Priest, but Fr. Nikodemos did not say anything to me, and I was just a simple monk under obedience. I could not do anything without obedience, not even go make an additional prostration.

I made a prostration to my elder and then bowed my head from afar towards the Great High Priest. Moving backwards, without turning my back towards him, I left the room. Immediately, the interrogation began again. I saw then that all our life, our works, our words, and our thoughts are written down and we will have to give an account for all of those things. As far as my Elder, I was informed that his soul did very well.

Once, I begged God for the soul of the poor monk that reposed because of the burns he sustained over his whole body. I saw him in a spiritual manner, and he was not at rest. I said to him:

"How are you, Father. How is it going?"

"I am not at rest," he said to me.

"Why, Father, are you not at rest?"

Then he proceeded to tell me about a particular event that I had forgotten about:

> One time, when I was passing by the fountain, you were washing some vegetables and I did not greet you. Then you said to me, "Father, why didn't you say hello to me? Could you say, 'Good day'?"
>
> "I didn't wish you 'Good day,' because it isn't written in Holy Scriptures, is what I snapped back at you, Fr. Iakovos."
>
> "Well, then what word is there?"
>
> "There is the word 'Hail'."
>
> "Well, then use that word."
>
> " 'No' I scoffed at you. 'I won't say that to you; I hate you.' That's what I said and then left, so now I am not at rest."

This same monk appeared to me and to my elder several times asking for help. I always commemorated him at the Divine Liturgy, but my elder also encouraged me to do *trisagia*. My elder also told me to go after the Divine Liturgy, fully vested, to that brother's grave and read special prayers to bring peace to his soul. After doing all of this, I saw him once outside of a great palace just before twilight. He was running very quickly with a lamp in his hand to go buy oil. I asked him, "What are you doing, father?"

"Leave me alone; don't slow me down. I am going to buy oil." Then, I don't know how, I told him, "My father, now it is late and they have already closed the door. They are not selling oil; you should have bought some when it was open." Then I saw him get lost in the deep darkness of the path.

There was once a lawyer from Chalkida that was the representative for the legal cases involving the monasteries, including ours. He would deal with cases for things like trespassing on properties, and so on. Even though we were so poor, we collected a little money—10, 20, or 50 drachmas—when people would make donations and we would somehow make from that 20, 30, or 50,000 drachmas that we would give to him to be our attorney. Eventually that lawyer died. I thought to myself, "Where did his soul go?"

I saw him and said to him, "Mr. *So and So*, how are you? How are things going?"

Then he told me, "Oh, Fr. Iakovos—I am having to give a big account for my cases—I still haven't gotten to your monastery yet. I am being examined for the cases I worked on for St. Nicholas at Galataki."

His soul was in great agony.

There was a shepherd that had a deep hatred in his soul. What did he do? Well, he went secretly to the animals of a fellow shepherd—a man that he hated—and he stabbed his animals with long skewers and left them like that. In a few days, those poor animals died. And then that shepherd, who was full of hatred, died; and where his soul went, there is no light.

Another time, I saw my own father sitting outside of a small, simple house like a cell and I said to him:

> "My father, you worked in construction: you didn't build yourself a larger house to enjoy, but you are sitting in such a small house?"
>
> He replied, "My child, you built this house for me to stay in only through your prayers and alms."

THE NARROW AND DIFFICULT PATH

One time, when I was reading the Gospel, I read the phrase: "Because narrow is the gate and difficult is the way that leads to life."[31] I said, "What is this way?" Then I was taken in a spiritual manner to a place where there was a very narrow path, like a tube, and I had to go into it. I wondered, "How could a person fit through there? They would be squeezed." Then I tried to go forward with unbearable difficulty, pulling myself forward with my hands and feet until I made it through that fearsome path. Only my elder and I were able to pass through this way.

Another time I found myself before a giant abyss, a bottomless chasm. Across this abyss there was a golden-white bridge that was no wider than a finger and I had to pass over this bridge to the other side. I made my way onto the bridge, walking very slowly and carefully, because if I fell into that chasm I surely would be lost. It was truly a struggle to do this; and then, suddenly, the golden bridge started to swing dangerously and to shake, putting me in danger of falling. I turned to see who was rocking the bridge, and what did I see? I saw the faces of some of the other fathers of the monastery rocking the bridge, and I asked them, "Fathers, why are you shaking the bridge? Don't you see that if I fall into this abyss I will die?" In any case, I had passed over the great length of the bridge and had a only little bit left to get to the other side.

A SENSE OF HUMOR

The Elder was most graceful when telling comedic stories, and he would even imitate the voices of the people he was talking about. Here is one:

---

31 Matthew 7:14.

There was a poor woman that served in a church nearby as a sexton. The poor thing had the bad habit of drinking wine and, little by little, it became a passion. She would drink the wine for the church that was used for Holy Communion. One time she was getting the church ready and there was no more wine in the closet; and the old woman, very upset, went in front of the icon of the Mother of God, begging for help. Not knowing that the priest was standing in the altar, she said:

> "My Panagia, please enlighten some good Christian person to bring a little wine so that I have some to drink."

The priest heard her and stood behind the icon of Panagia in the altar and replied:

> "Don't drink wine! You don't need to drink wine."

The old woman, thinking that it was the child Jesus replying from the arms of Panagia, responded,

> "Shush, you! Don't talk; you're a child. I am talking to your mother. I'm asking your mother for help."

Spiritual Sight

One of the Elder's spiritual children came to him and asked for his help regarding a certain monk who had lived in a community for several years. Without a blessing that monk had left to go live by himself in a cell. The Elder replied, "My child, I see the demons dancing around him."

Another time, one of the Elder's spiritual children came to him and said, "We went to the monastery of St. Dionysios of Olympus." The Elder replied, completely naturally, "My child, St. Dionysios was here a few days ago and we celebrated the Divine Liturgy together."

There was a time when a certain woman became possessed by a demon and her children brought her to the monastery. They asked the Elder, "Maybe she got possessed by a demon because she prayed too much?" St. Iakovos replied, "My children, prayer does not make someone become possessed by a demon. But maybe your mother was prideful, maybe she thought she was a holy person? Perhaps that is why God allowed her to become possessed by a demon."

The Elder told another story: "One time we were gathering wood for the monastery with a truck, and Fr. Kyrillos[32] went to help. I told him, 'Fr. Kyrillos: be careful that nothing bad happens to you, because I saw a demon running on top of the truck, on top of the wood. Don't lose an eye!' At the end of the work, a piece of wood fell off and hit Fr. Kyrillos in the eye very badly and it gave him many problems before it finally healed."

WARS

The Elder would frequently visit the relics of St. John the Russian, especially when he was going to Athens for medical appointments.

> One time I saw the saint alive in his glass casket and I said to him, "My saint, how were things in Asia Minor? What virtues did you have that led to your sanctification?"

---

32 He became the abbot of the monastery of St. David after St. Iakovos. (TN)

The saint replied, "I slept inside of a cave that was used as a stable, on top of straw which I would use to cover myself during the winter so I would not be cold. I had humility and faith."

Saint John continued, "Wait a second, Fr. Iakovos, because two people just came to me asking for help with a sick child. Wait here while I go help them."

Suddenly, the casket was empty. After a little while, the saint returned. I didn't see how he returned but I saw him straightening out his clothes in the casket. Then I said to him, "My saint, you have a lot of pilgrims that come here to venerate your relics."

The saint replied, "Fr. Iakovos, you have no idea what is going on in the world. Evil and sin have advanced very much, and things are still getting worse. There must be a war, there must be a war, there must be a war."

The saint said this three times.

One of the Elder's spiritual children asked him, "Elder, when will there be a war?" The Elder replied, "All of the car accidents that happen around here, that isn't a war?" That was his only reply.

The Elder's Mansion

One time, I was reading the life of St. Seraphim of Sarov and I got to the point where the saint describes how he saw the dwellings of Paradise: "in my Father's house there are many mansions."[33] I thought to myself, "What are those houses like?" All of a sudden, the book fell out of my hands, and I was taken to a place that was most beautiful. In front

---

33 John 14:2.

of me was a road planted with violets, all the same color, densely clustered together and giving off a sweet fragrance. And standing next to me was an old monk; it was St. David.

I wanted to go forward, but I hesitated because I did not want to step on the flowers. I asked, "Who planted these so close together? If there was a little opening, I could put my feet in between them and not crush any of them."

Then St. David said to me, "Go on, go on. Keep going, Fr. Iakovos: don't worry about the flowers. They are not like the ones that you know; they won't get broken."

I kept going, and when I stepped on the flowers they did not become crushed. I saw to my right an unimaginably steep path going down. It was a dangerous dirt path, and I asked St. David, "What is that road going down? If a car were to try and go there it would be in great danger."

The saint replied, "Fr. Iakovos, here there are no cars. Forget about that road; don't even look at it. You keep going on the road you are going now."

We continued down the flower-covered road, and I decided to look around at what else there was.

I saw the most beautiful houses, spread out like palaces with their fences and gates. Everything was full of flowers, beauty, and light, but they were completely empty. There was not a single person in them. Then I said to St. David, who was still walking along with me: "Elder, what silence and beauty is this? If only I could have a house like that to sit in silence and pray because I am a man of spiritual silence."

St. David held up his hand and showed me the house that was for me. Suddenly I found myself back in my cell and said,

"Why did I come back to this world? If only I hadn't returned but could have stayed there forever!"

\+ + +

O Lord Jesus Christ, would that through the prayers of Father Iakovos you will grant to all of us, who had the blessing to know Your servant, that when we leave this temporary life we may live in those celestial mansions through the intercessions of St. David and all of the saints, especially the intercessions of Your All-Spotless Mother, as we proclaim imploringly: Through the prayers of the Holy Fathers, Lord Jesus Christ Our God, have mercy on us and save us.

Ἱερὰ Μονὴ ὁσίου Δαυίδ τῇ 20/11/1991

Κυρία Δήμητρα χαῖρε ἐν Κυρίῳ πάντοτε.
Ἔλαβον τὸ γράμμα σου, τὰ ὀνόματα πάντων καὶ κεκοιμημένων καὶ τὸ τσὲκ 220 δολλάρια δεχθῶς σᾶς εὐχαριστῶ δι' ὅλα. Τὰς εὐχὰς σας τὸν σεβασμὸν καὶ τὴν χαρὰ σας χαίρω, ἔχει ἄνωθεν πνευματικά, καὶ πως τὸ ἅγιον Μοναστῆρι μνημονεύομεν τὰ ὀνόματά σας ὑπὲρ ὑγείας σας σωτηρίας καὶ παντὸς ἀγαθοῦ, καὶ τῶν κεκοιμημένων σας ὑπὲρ ἀναπαύσεως. Ποτέ μου δὲν σᾶς ξεχνῶ εἰς προσευχές μου πάντοτε σᾶς θυμᾶμαι καὶ δεόμεθα διὰ τὴν οἰκογένεια σου τὸν φίλιππον καὶ τὰ παιδιά σου Νικόλαον, Ἐλευθέριον καὶ Δημήτριον νὰ τὰ σκεπάζῃ ἡ χάρις τοῦ Θεοῦ νὰ τὰ εὐλογεῖ καὶ νὰ τὰ διαφυλάττῃ ἀπὸ κάθε κακό, καὶ γιὰ τὸν πατὲρ Ἐφραὶμ δεόμεθα νὰ τὸν χαρίζῃ ὁ θεὸς χρόνια γιὰ τὸ καλὸ τὰς ψυχῶν μας. Διαβιβάζε σὰς παρακαλῶ κατὰ τὴν εὐλογίαν τοῦ ὁσίου Δαυὶδ εἰς τὸν σύζυγόν σας φίλιππον καὶ παιδιά, εἰς πνευματικὲς χεῖρες σας καὶ πρόσφερον τὰ δῶρα τους εἰς τὸ Μοναστῆρι. Σᾶς εὔχομαι ὑγείαν χαρὰν καὶ τὰς ἄγαθα καὶ εὐλογίαν οὐρανιον καλὴ Τεσσαρακοστὴ καὶ καλὰ Χριστοὺ Γέννα, καὶ καλὴν χρονία.
Μετ' εὐχῶν καὶ ἀγάπης Χριστοῦ
Ἱερομ. Π. Ἰάκωβος
ὁ Χριστὸς μαζί σας

UNCUT MOUNTAIN PRESS TITLES

Books by Archpriest Peter Heers

Fr. Peter Heers, *The Ecclesiological Renovation of Vatican II: An Orthodox Examination of Rome's Ecumenical Theology Regarding Baptism and the Church*, 2015

Fr. Peter Heers, *The Missionary Origins of Modern Ecumenism: Milestones Leading up to 1920*, 2007

The Works of our Father Among the Saints, Nikodemos the Hagiorite

Vol. 1: *Exomologetarion: A Manual of Confession*
Vol. 2: *Concerning Frequent Communion of the Immaculate Mysteries of Christ*
Vol. 3: *Confession of Faith*

Other Available Titles

Elder Cleopa of Romania, *The Truth of Our Faith*
Elder Cleopa of Romania, *The Truth of Our Faith, Vol. II*
Fr. John Romanides, *Patristic Theology: The University Lectures of Fr. John Romanides*
Demetrios Aslanidis and Monk Damascene Grigoriatis, *Apostle to Zaire: The Life and Legacy of Blessed Father Cosmas of Grigoriou*
Protopresbyter Anastasios Gotsopoulos, *On Common Prayer with the Heterodox According to the Canons of the Church*
Robert Spencer, *The Church and the Pope*
G. M. Davis, *Antichrist: The Fulfillment of Globalization*
Athonite Fathers of the 20th Century, Vol. I
St. Gregory Palamas, *Apodictic Treatises on the Procession of the Holy Spirit*
St. Hilarion Troitsky, *On the Dogma of the Church: An Historical Overview of the Sources of Ecclesiology*
Fr. Alexander Webster and Fr. Peter Heers, Editors, *Let No One Fear Death*
Subdeacon Nektarios Harrison, *Metropolitan Philaret of New York*
Elder George of Grigoriou, *Catholicism in the Light of Orthodoxy*
Archimandrite Ephraim Triandaphillopoulos, *Noetic Prayer as the Basis of Mission and the Struggle Against Heresy*
On the Reception of the Heterodox into the Orthodox Church: The Patristic Consensus and Criteria

Select Forthcoming Titles

The Orthodox Patristic Witness Concerning Catholicism
Georgio, *Errors of the Latins*
Fr. Peter Heers, *Going Deeper in the Spiritual Life*
Abbe Guette, *The Papacy*
Athonite Fathers of the 20th Century, Vol. II

This 1ˢᵗ Edition of
LIFE AND WITNESS OF ST. IAKOVOS OF EVIA

written by Dr. Nicholas Baldimtsis, translated by Fr. Nicholas Metrakos, with a cover design by George Weis, typeset in Baskerville, printed in this two thousand and twenty-third year of our Lord's Holy Incarnation is one of the many fine titles available from Uncut Mountain Press, translators and publishers of Orthodox Christian theological and spiritual literature. Find the book you are looking for at

uncutmountainpress.com

**GLORY BE TO GOD
FOR ALL THINGS**

AMEN.

www.ingramcontent.com/pod-product-compliance
Lightning Source LLC
Chambersburg PA
CBHW060405080526
44583CB00012B/474